THE
HISTORY OF
AFGHANISTAN

ADVISORY BOARD

THE
HISTORY OF
AFGHANISTAN

Meredith L. Runion

The Greenwood Histories of the Modern Nations
Frank W. Thackeray and John E. Findling, Series Editors

Greenwood Press
Westport, Connecticut • London

Library of Congress Cataloging-in-Publication Data

Runion, Meredith L.
    The history of Afghanistan / by Meredith L. Runion.
        p. cm. — (Greenwood histories of the modern nations, ISSN 1096–2905)
    Includes bibliographical references and index.
    ISBN 978–0–313–33798–7 (alk. paper)
    1. Afghanistan—History.   I. Title.
    DS356.R86   2007
    958.1—dc22   2007026934

British Library Cataloguing in Publication Data is available.

Library of Congress Catalog Card Number: 2007026934
ISBN-13: 978–0–313–33798–7
ISSN: 1096–2905

First published in 2007

Greenwood Press, 88 Post Road West, Westport, CT 06881
An imprint of Greenwood Publishing Group, Inc.
www.greenwood.com

Printed in the United States of America

The paper used in this book complies with the
Permanent Paper Standard issued by the National
Information Standards Organization (Z39.48–1984).

10 9 8 7 6 5 4 3 2 1

To Mom, Dad, Courtney, and Kory—With love.

To Casey—My memories of you will live forever,
and it saddens me you could not.

This book is also dedicated to the women and
children of Afghanistan.

History is indeed the witness of the times, the light of truth.

—Marcus Cicero

Whoever wishes to foresee the future must consult the past; for human events ever resemble those of preceding times. This arises from the fact that they are produced by men who ever have been, and ever shall be, animated by the same passions, and thus they necessarily have the same results.

—Niccolo Machiavelli

Contents

Series Foreword

The *Greenwood Histories of the Modern Nations* series is intended to provide students and interested laypeople with up-to-date, concise, and analytical histories of many of the nations of the contemporary world. Not since the 1960s has there been a systematic attempt to publish a series of national histories, and, as editors, we believe that this series will prove to be a valuable contribution to our understanding of other countries in our increasingly interdependent world.

More than 30 years ago, at the end of the 1960s, the Cold War was an accepted reality of global politics, the process of decolonization was still in progress, the idea of a unified Europe with a single currency was unheard of, the United States was mired in a war in Vietnam, and the economic boom of Asia was still years in the future. Richard Nixon was president of the United States, Mao Tse-tung (not yet Mao Zedong) ruled China, Leonid Brezhnev guided the Soviet Union, and Harold Wilson was prime minister of the United Kingdom. Authoritarian dictators still ruled most of Latin America, the Middle East was reeling in the wake of the Six-Day War, and Shah Reza Pahlavi was at the height of his power in Iran. Clearly, the past 30 years have been witness to a great deal of historical change, and it is to this change that this series is primarily addressed.

With the help of a distinguished advisory board, we have selected nations whose political, economic, and social affairs mark them as among the most important in the waning years of the twentieth century, and for each nation we have found an author who is recognized as a specialist in the history of that nation. These authors have worked most cooperatively with us and with Greenwood Press to produce volumes that reflect current research on their nations and that are interesting and informative to their prospective readers.

The importance of a series such as this cannot be underestimated. As a superpower whose influence is felt all over the world, the United States can claim a "special" relationship with almost every other nation. Yet many Americans know very little about the histories of the nations with which the United States relates. How did they get to be the way they are? What kind of political systems have evolved there? What kind of influence do they have in their own region? What are the dominant political, religious, and cultural forces that move their leaders? These and many other questions are answered in the volumes of this series.

The authors who have contributed to this series have written comprehensive histories of their nations, dating back to prehistoric times in some cases. Each of them, however, has devoted a significant portion of the book to events of the last 30 years, because the modern era has contributed the most to contemporary issues that have an impact on U.S. policy. Authors have made an effort to be as up-to-date as possible so that readers can benefit from the most recent scholarship and a narrative that includes very recent events.

In addition to the historical narrative, each volume in this series contains an introductory overview of the country's geography, political institutions, economic structure, and cultural attributes. This is designed to give readers a picture of the nation as it exists in the contemporary world. Each volume also contains additional chapters that add interesting and useful detail to the historical narrative. One chapter is a thorough chronology of important historical events, making it easy for readers to follow the flow of a particular nation's history. Another chapter features biographical sketches of the nation's most important figures to humanize some of the individuals who have contributed to the historical development of their nation. Each volume also contains a comprehensive bibliography, so that those readers whose interest has been sparked may find out more about the nation and its history. Finally, there is a carefully prepared topic and person index.

Readers of these volumes will find them fascinating to read and useful in understanding the contemporary world and the nations that compose it. As series editors, it is our hope that this series will contribute to a heightened sense of global understanding as we embark on a new century.

Frank W. Thackeray and John E. Findling
Indiana University Southeast

Acknowledgments

Compiling the history of Afghanistan is without question an enormous task. In some instances, there can be a multitude of information with conflicting facts and dates and differing timelines of events. Each historian has his or her own perspective and opinion on past events, which quite often may be completely contradictory to the recorded accounts of another author. Very little is written about Afghanistan's prehistory, while libraries and bookstores are filled with a multitude of works on the early life of Mesopotamia and Persia. Further, most books provide only one or two paragraphs on the early civilization era of Afghanistan, usually after Alexander the Great conquered the region of Afghanistan. As a result, the completion of this book has been an endless adventure in the quest for the events that created Afghanistan as it is today. Clearly, writing a work of this magnitude with such an encompassing scope and time span created long hours of research, and I could not have accomplished this without much-needed support from family and friends. I offer my sincere thanks to the many friends and colleagues whose personal assistance helped me complete this book. My deepest gratitude belongs to my sister, the one who encouraged me on this endeavor. Your countless suggestions, assistance, and wisdom helped me through those difficult writing times. I also would like to thank my parents for their hard work and sacrifices over the years, and I appreciate your continuous support and encouragement to steer me onto the right path in life. I offer special thanks to my best friend, Kory Embrey, by far my greatest and most playful critic, and without your support, this book simply could not have been completed. I offer my gratitude to Glenn for your support and encouragement. I also would like to thank my godfather, author Dr. Robert Shumaker, who has always encouraged me to reach beyond my potential. I offer heartfelt thanks to all my family for the countless times of support and encouragement while completing this work.

To my friends and colleagues at work, my debt and gratitude to all of you cannot be expressed in only a few words. Your inspiration and words of encouragement made me believe in myself. I am indebted and offer my sincere gratitude to Dan, a great coworker and true friend who believed in me and encouraged me throughout the completion of this book. I sincerely thank my close friends Efrain, Dawn, and Gilles for your constant encouragement, and I would especially like to thank Jennifer for your remarkable friendship, guidance, and support. Additionally, I would like to thank my friends Kim, Mary Ann, Celeste, and Todd for your professional support and encouragement throughout this endeavor. Thank you to my friends Tomas, Travis, Patti, Tom, and Patrick for making the office a great place to work. I offer sincere thanks and the utmost respect to all of my colleagues in the government, and I thank all of those who are not mentioned here but will be thanked individually. Thank you to my friend Jason for your words of inspiration and encouragement, and I cannot begin to describe how grateful I am to have you as a close friend.

Many thanks to the Fairfax County Public Library System for your assistance and recommendations of books to research, and special thanks to the Library of Congress in Washington, D.C. I also would like to thank the many authors and historians who were brave enough to write and publish books on Afghanistan. My sincere thanks and recognition for your masterpieces are included in the works referenced. I hope others will enjoy reading your hard work as much as I did while researching this book. Last but not least, I would like to offer my deepest gratitude to Greenwood Press for publishing the all-encompassing History of Afghanistan and especially my editor Sarah Colwell for your patience, and additional thanks to Apex Publishing for your support on this project.

In the future, if you perhaps encounter a writer in the midst of working on a nonfiction book, especially one on the history of the world, please look upon them with kind eyes and offer words of encouragement. They need it.

SPELLING AND TERMINOLOGY

Writing about countries in the Middle East and Central Asia is quite a daunting task. Name variations are plentiful, and often searching for one word just leads you to another variation. This book contains references to other common spellings, and the list of variations is seemingly endless. Please forgive any oversight or errors on my part.

Timeline

The following displays a chronological outline of the major events and significant dates in the history of Afghanistan.

3000–2000 B.C.E.	The first true urban dwellings rise in two areas of Afghanistan.
2000–1500 B.C.E.	The current capital of Afghanistan, Kabul, was established as a city.
550–331 B.C.E.	Afghanistan subjected to rule under the Achaemenid dynasty.
500 B.C.E.	King Darius I conquers the region of Afghanistan.
331–327 B.C.E.	Alexander the Great invades and conquers the region of Afghanistan.
255 B.C.E.	Emperor Asoka introduces Buddhism to Afghanistan.
150 B.C.E.–A.D. 300	Five merging tribes unite under the Kushan tribe, thus beginning the Kushan Empire.
400	Invasion by the Hepthalites (White Huns) that leaves Afghanistan in ruins.

570	Birth of the Prophet Muhammad, the founder of the Islamic faith.
642–652	The Arabs introduce Islam to Afghanistan and rename the region Khurasan.
962–1030	Afghanistan becomes the center of Islamic power and civilization under the Ghaznavid Empire.
1186–1219	Rule of the Ghorid dynasty in Afghanistan.
1219	Genghis Khan invades and conquers Afghanistan, killing thousands and leaving Afghanistan in ruins.
1370–1506	Mongol conqueror Timor-e-Lang defeats Afghanistan and leaves the region in destruction and begins the rule of the Timurid dynasty.
1506–1747	Afghanistan is split between the Moghul and Safavid empires.
1722	The Afghans invade Persia and overthrow the Safavid Empire.
1736	Nadir assumes power as shah by expelling the Afghans from Persia.
1747	Nadir Shah is assassinated, and Ahmad Shah Abdali (assuming the name Ahmad Shah Durrani) establishes modern Afghanistan.
1747–1773	Rule of Ahmad Shah Durrani, known as the "Father of Afghanistan."
1773–1793	Rule of Timur Shah Durrani. During this time, the capital of Afghanistan transferred from Kandahar to Kabul because of tribal opposition.
1793–1801	Rule of Zaman Shah Durrani.
1795	Persians invade the province of Khuasan.
1801–1803	Rule of Shah Mahmood Durrani during constant internal revolts in Afghanistan.
1803–1809	Rule of Shah Shuja.
1809–1818	Shah Mahmood returns to the throne and leads a war with Persia.

1819–1826	The sons of Timur Shah fight and struggle to seize the throne during a period of Afghan civil war.
1834–1839	Dost Mohammad Khan takes Kabul and establishes control over Afghanistan.
1839	British troops invade Afghanistan.
1839–1842	First Anglo-Afghan War.
1839–1842	Shah Shuja is appointed king by the British and is killed in April 1842 by the Afghans.
1843–1846	Rule of Akbar Khan.
1846–1863	The once-exiled Dost Mohammad Khan returns to occupy the throne.
1878–1880	Second Anglo-Afghan War.
1893	Abdur Rahman signs the Durand Line agreement with the British.
1919	Third and final Anglo-Afghan War.
1919	Afghanistan declares political independence from the United Kingdom and becomes an independent state in the Treaty of Rawalpindi. August 19 is commemorated as Afghanistan's Independence Day.
1931	The new Constitution of Afghanistan signed on October 31.
1946	Afghanistan is admitted to the United Nations.
1973	King Zahir Shah is overthrown and forced into exile, and the new ruler, Prime Minister Mohammed Daoud, declares Afghanistan a republic.
1979	Military invasion by the Soviet Union and the start of the Soviet Afghan War that would continue for 10 years.
1989	Soviet forces withdraw from Afghanistan.
1992	Collapse of the communist regime by mujahideen forces.
1994	A radical Islamic group known as the Taliban establishes a campaign to overthrow Afghanistan. The Taliban capture the city of Kandahar.
1995	The Taliban seize control of Herat.

1996	The Taliban seize Kabul and most of the country.
September 2001	The World Trade Center in New York City and the Pentagon in Washington, D.C., are attacked by airplanes hijacked by terrorists.
October 2001	The United States invades Afghanistan.
January 2004	Loya Jirga participants adopt the Afghan Constitution.
October 9, 2004	First Afghan presidential election in which more than 8.1 million Afghans participate.
December 7, 2004	The inauguration of Hamid Karzai as the first democratically elected president of Afghanistan.

Map of Afghanistan.

1

An Introduction to Afghanistan: The Land and People

Since the dawn of humankind and throughout history, Afghanistan has faced centuries of turmoil and strife. Only in recent years has the country been able to rebuild from the destructive and seemingly constant warfare that has plagued this land. Afghanistan's history is one steeped in conflict, distress, and social unrest but nonetheless offers a wide-ranging, intriguing, and diverse narrative. Because of the country's location along the crucial trade routes between Asia and the Middle East, Afghanistan has been repeatedly invaded and conquered by rulers and foreign governments for centuries. Yet none of these invaders have successfully sustained a lasting foothold in the country, and as such, gaining control in the rugged and challenging terrain of Afghanistan is fleeting at best. For these prevailing empires, it should have been an ominous warning when the newly conquering army erected magnificent monoliths on the crumbled ruins of previously defeated empires. As history has proven, triumphant victory in Afghanistan should be considered only a temporary feat, for success will be taken almost as quickly as it was given.

In 2001, the U.S. military toppled the al-Qaeda regime and released modern Afghanistan from the control of the Taliban. For many Afghan citizens, democratic hope was solidified when the country held elections in October 2004 that allowed Afghanistan to become an Islamic republic. This new democratically elected government seeks to unite and reconstruct Afghanistan, but the road to recovery will not be easy—Afghanistan faces numerous obstacles, such as a rebuilding a crumbled economy, eliminating the continued opium drug trafficking (which is credited as the largest income source in the country), obliterating the country's large den of terrorist activity, recovering buried land mines from constant wars, and assisting with the return home for millions of refugees after years of exile. This newly elected government has the arduous task of transforming this war-torn country into a land of peace and prosperity in the 21st century. In this regard, many companies are reluctant to invest in such a troubled and problematic nation, but Afghanistan desperately needs this income to increase and stabilize the economy. While the current visualizations of Afghanistan may generate images of extremely rocky mountains and arid deserts with sparse vegetation, it is hard to imagine that once upon a time, Afghanistan was a land of paradise with lush foliage that made this region one of the most beautiful locations in the world. Despite current topographical conditions, it is the hope of the newly elected assembly that the world will one day recognize Afghanistan as a land of optimism, freedom, and new beginnings.

GEOGRAPHY

Afghanistan is an entirely landlocked country located in southern Asia and is located to the east of Iran and both north and west of Pakistan. Other countries making up the border include Turkmenistan, Uzbekistan, and Tajikistan. On the eastern side of the country, Afghanistan also shares a small section of the border with China. Afghanistan has a total land area of roughly 250,000 square miles (652,000 square kilometers) and is frequently referenced as being slightly smaller than the state of Texas. The topography of Afghanistan is divided primarily into three regions: the pastoral farmland in the north, the central highlands in the middle section of the country (including the majority of the Hindu Kush Mountains), and the mostly barren and windswept desert of the southern plateau.

The far northern terrain is the country's main agricultural region and is composed mostly of fertile grassy plains, cultivated fields, and rolling hills. The northern plains are a highly populated agricultural area where farmers cultivate such agricultural products as wheat, rice, and cotton. Shepherds and pastoral herders raise livestock such as sheep and goats in the grassy regions. This northeastern area of Afghanistan stretches approximately 40,000 square miles from the central highlands to the Iran–Tajikistan border. However, this fertile area still requires an adequate water source to allow for optimum cultivation and crop harvest since annual rainfall is scarce. Because of this shortfall, this lush farm region comprises only about 12 percent of the total land area in the entire country. Not only has drought taken a toll on the once-fertile soil, but land mines are scattered throughout the region as well. Afghanistan has served as the battleground for many wars, and these land mines are a token of war from the decade-long conflict of the Soviet invasion in 1979. These impeding factors make farming increasingly difficult for the Afghans who toil to make a living off the terrain. In addition, the cropland that was once used for wheat is now used primarily for poppy cultivation since for these farmers harvesting wheat, rice, and corn does not compare to the profits received from the lucrative drug-smuggling business. As a result, Afghanistan relies largely on importing products, and traditionally the import totals have routinely exceeded the amount of exported products.

The second region, known as the central highlands, encompasses the majority of Afghanistan and covers an area of approximately 160,000 square miles. By far the most prominent geographic feature in Afghanistan are the large mountain ranges that are part of the Himalayan Mountains. These long mountain series cover nearly two-thirds of the country and stretch from China into central Afghanistan. This famously rough and rugged landscape is referred to as the Hindu Kush Mountains, which is just one of several mountain chains in Afghanistan. The literal translation of the name "Hindu Kush" is a true reflection of its harsh terrain, as this difficult and jagged section of Afghanistan translates to "Killer of Hindus." For the most part, the central highlands experience desert–steppe types of soil, but snowfall is a typical weather condition in the mountains. Further, erosion is apparent in the mountainous areas that are affected by monsoons and heavy precipitation.

As a natural result of the earth's shifting tectonic plates that form these mountain ranges, this area is prone to large earthquakes. Yet even with this treacherous and unstable terrain, the deep valleys and high mountains have played a vital role in the struggle for control of Afghanistan, and as such this region has been important to the defense of the country. The Hindu Kush range is approximately 230 square miles (600 square kilometers) in length and stretches from Kabul westward. Other prominent ranges include the northwestward Torkestan Mountains, the Siah Kuh range, the northern-reaching Hesar Mountains, and the southwestern-reaching ranges of the Malmand and Khakbad mountains. The Wakhan Corridor is an extremely narrow piece of land in the Badakhshan region of Afghanistan, located in the far north of the country. This small section of land in the Pamir Mountain region stretches out from the country like a tentacle toward China. Located between Tajikistan and Pakistan, the British Empire established the Wakhan Corridor at the end of the 19th century to be used as a buffer area against Russia's quest for expansion into India during the period of "The Great Game." At the far eastern end of the corridor, the Wakjir is a narrow passageway through the Hindu Kush. This precarious thoroughfare is closed for five months of the year due to weather conditions, and is often theorized as an infrequent location for drug smuggling from Afghanistan into China.

The third region is a dry and arid desert plateau that makes up the southwestern area of Afghanistan, close to Pakistan and Iran. This mostly infertile desert is referred to as the southern plateau and comprises nearly 50,000 square miles. Several rivers cross the plateau, allowing for some fertile soil to thrive near the river's alluvial deposits. The largest river in Afghanistan is the Helmand River, which begins in the Hindu Kush Mountains, runs through the southern desert region, and ends along the border with Iran. As the principal river in the southwestern region and only 715 miles in length, the Helmand is an important geographic feature and serves an imperative function for the country. The river and its tributaries operate as a major drainage source for more than 100,000 square miles of Afghanistan.

Afghanistan has an abundance of natural resources, including natural gas, petroleum, coal, sulfur, and both precious and semiprecious stones. In addition, mineral resources are in great quantity and include chrome, copper, gold, iron, lead, salt, and silver. The northern region is extremely fertile and contains a large amount of the country's minerals and natural gas deposits. The largest export is salt, with nearly 40,000 tons of salt being mined each year. However, the country's source of opium ranks the highest in the world, with over 75 percent of the world's opium coming from Afghanistan.[1]

A land of stark contrasts, Afghanistan experiences extremely cold winters in the northern mountains and endures incredibly hot summer temperatures in the southwestern desert. The dry and arid time of the year is primarily June to September, but even during these hot days, the nights can become very cold. The mountain ranges also face temperature contrasts, as the northern mountain ranges experience frigid arctic weather conditions, yet the eastern mountain ranges experience the sultry outcome of neighboring regions. These eastern mountains close to the Pakistan border endure the aftereffects of the Indian monsoons, and these areas experience more rainfall and stronger winds than other sections of the country. In these mountainous areas, the climate reaches tropical temperatures and often high humidity and windy rains. As a result of this humid climate, the vegetation and plant life are extremely lush and fruitful. In complete opposite, the land of the southwestern desert region is extremely dry and barren, and strong winds contribute to frequent sandstorms. As such, vegetation and plant life are present but only as desolate freckles on the face of this sandy desert. Not surprisingly, annual rainfall is scarce in Afghanistan, with region totals varying from approximately three inches in the barren city of Farah to up to 50 inches per year in the mountains. Records show the greatest extent of precipitation recorded is 53 inches of rain in the Salang Pass of the Hindu Kush. The capital city of Kabul, located in the mideastern region, experiences relatively normal temperatures, but the climate of Afghanistan is not one of human luxury. In this regard, the climate extremes and the rough terrain further Afghanistan's paradox as a land of desolate differences.

ECONOMY

From an economic perspective, Afghanistan is considered one of the poorest and least developed countries in the world. Categorized as a Third World country, Afghanistan ranks number 250 out of 300 countries in economic status. Since Afghanistan is a landlocked country and thereby does not have direct access to seaports, the country must rely on economic partnerships with such countries as Pakistan, the United States, and India for imports and exports.[2] Furthermore, the severe turmoil that has occurred over the past 25 years has not been particularly beneficial for Afghanistan's economy. This crippling of the country's financial market clearly began with the Soviet invasion in 1979 and would continue under the Soviets' 10-year occupational struggle for the control of Afghanistan. During this fierce rivalry and incursion, Afghanistan's economy was severely devastated, and the successive economic impacts of the Taliban and mujahideen governments forced the economy into a rigid state of collapse. To this day in modern Afghanistan, the economy has yet to recover fully from years of devastation and disintegration. Yet for many countries, Afghanistan is regarded as the key to social and economic development, stability, and growth for this region of the world. Surrounding countries, such as China, Pakistan, Iran, and Russia, look toward Afghanistan as the guiding light of the future, and all countries have at one point played a guiding role in the trade and political structure of the country.[3] As a further impediment, chemical weapons that were used during the Afghan war with the Soviets caused severe damage to the country's environment and ecosystem. The recent drought from 1998 to 2001 further hindered the struggling economy and added to the nation's rapidly expanding problems. Yet there is some hope on the horizon that since the fall of the Taliban in December 2001, the economy of Afghanistan has improved. However, this financial growth is not advancing quickly enough, and, regrettably, any economic progress for the country is slow moving.[4]

In modern times and throughout the 1990s, the country's largest revenue source was a result of illegal drug smuggling. Afghanistan is the world's leading opiate producer, and the high drug sales indicate that the opium poppy is undoubtedly Afghanistan's most profitable crop. Opium is harvested from the poppies grown in the fertile northern mountain region, and during the 1990s, the profitable market for producing and smuggling illegal drugs was more alluring than the traditional pastoral efforts. On the one-eighth of the land area in Afghanistan that once grew such crops as wheat, corn, and rice,

the farmers now cultivate the soil with poppies for opium and heroin. Ironically, the Taliban regime was largely successful in eliminating the farming of
these illegal substances, of which the farmers received little profit from the
sale of poppy cultivation. After the Taliban's collapse, the provisional government continued to eliminate the illegal drug trade that was mostly continued
through the large opium reserves in the country. Corruption and bribery still
allow the trade to continue.

Since the fall of the Taliban, opium production has steadily risen again,
with recent figures doubling the sale and production of opium from 2002,
and estimates show that 3,600 tons of opium were cultivated in Afghanistan
in 2003. This is a difficult conundrum for President Karzai, as funding from
the drug trade provides financial support for some of the major obstacles in
Afghanistan's economy, including warlords, existing members of the Taliban,
and corrupted government officials. Yet for the struggling farmers, producing
opium can yield up to 200 times more income than cultivating wheat, rice, and
corn. While trying to eliminate the drug trade, many argue that eradicating
this source of income for the farmers without providing a substitute income
and benefit will further impact the economy and the poverty in Afghanistan.
Perhaps even more challenging to the Karzai administration, a worldwide
sponsored program to pay farmers to destroy their opium fields was unsuccessful and resulted in money being given to the warlords and their supporters rather than to the farmers.[5] Thus opium and heroin production remains a
blossoming business in Afghanistan.

PEOPLE

The most recent figures as of June 2007 indicate that the population of Afghanistan is just over 31 million, with males representing 52 percent of the
population. These figures are rough estimates, as an official census has not
been held for more than 20 years in Afghanistan.[6] The people of Afghanistan
are comprised of a variety of ethnic groups, serving as evidence of the many
generations of invaders that have conquered and populated this land. Of
these ethnic groups, the Pashtuns make up nearly half of the population and
live in the southern and eastern regions of Afghanistan. The other three large
ethnic groups are the Tajiks, the Hazaras, and the Uzbeks, and minor ethnic
groups are the Aimak, the Turkmen, and the Baloch. These ethnic groups are
distinctly unique in their different cultural characteristics, such as family beliefs and languages. Afghanistan has two official languages, Pashtu and Dari
(Afghan Persi). As such, the Pashtuns speak Afghanistan's principal language
of Pashtu, while the Hazaras speak Dari (Persian). Recent U.S. government
estimates reveal that Dari is the main language among half of the population and that roughly 35 percent of the population speaks Pashtu (Pashto).

However, it is estimated that as many as 40 different languages are spoken in the country. These include the languages of the many ethnic groups in Afghanistan and include the Turkic languages among the Uzbek and Turkmen groups. Other language derivatives include those spoken by the Baluchi, the Pashai, and the Nuristani people.

As mentioned previously, the three regions of Afghanistan include the northern plains, the central highlands, and the southern plains. However, these segments can be further divided into general ethnic sections. The northern region, as divided by the Hindu Kush Mountains, may be separated into two ethic regions. These include the eastern region of the Badakhshan-Vakhan and the western region of the Balkh-Meymaneh. The Tajiks populate mainly the plateaus and mountains of the eastern region, and these tribal members work mostly as farmers, craftsman, and artisans. The Uzbeks and the Turkmen inhabit the plains of the western section and work mostly as farmers and herders in this highly fertile region.

The southern region of the Hindu Kush can further be divided into four regions named for the principal cities of Kabul, Kandahar, Herat, and Hazarajat. The Kabul region is located in the eastern section of the Hindu Kush and is the native soil of the Pashtun tribe, which includes both sedentary and nomadic sects. The Tajiks and the Nuristani also are indigenous to the Kabul region. The second region of the southern land of Afghanistan is the Kandahar region, which is populated by the Durrani Pashtun tribes. These tribes live around the city of Kandahar itself and are most noted for creating the central point of Afghanistan's social and political elite.[7] Additional inhabitants of the Kandahar region include the Balochi and Brahui peoples. The Herat region is the third subdivision and is populated by a combination of the Tajiks, the Pashtun, and the Chahar Aimak peoples. These ethnic groups reside mainly in the western region of Afghanistan. The fourth section, known as Hazarajat, is a mountainous region in the central highlands of Afghanistan, and for the most part the Hazara ethnic group populates this area. However, because of the scarceness of inhabitable territory, difficulty in communications, and the treacherous mountain terrain, many of the Hazara have moved to other, more habitable locations.

It is fascinating to note that even with such an expansive cultural diversity represented by a multitude of ethnic groups, this melting pot of cultures has not hindered the Afghans' ability to unite as a country and defend themselves against foreign invaders. This is a characteristic that has proven to be true in a 5,000-year history of constant invasion and warfare in this conflict-tattered land, for the Afghans are not only shepherds, farmers, and nomads but also intense fighters and fierce warriors. The differing ethnic backgrounds and languages still share a common religious belief in Islam, and it is this religious conviction that serves as the backbone for the population to aggressively resist foreign governments from trying to occupy their land. In this regard and throughout time, ownership and control of this region has proven to be only a temporary victory not only because of the harsh terrain and difficult climate but also because of the combative, resistant, and unbreakable nature of Afghanistan's population. The belief in Islam is a principal theme in the culture of the Afghans, as the Muslim faith can be found in every facet of life. The main religion of Afghanistan is overwhelmingly Sunni Muslim, comprising more than 80 percent of the population. Shi'a Muslim accounts for nearly all the remaining population, which includes the Hazara and the Kizilbash peoples. Previously, a small Jewish minority existed in the country before the Soviet invasion in 1979, but this population was forced out of Afghanistan. Throughout the late 1980s, almost one-third of the Afghanistan people were forced into exile as refugees. The majority of these refugees settled in Pakistan and Iran, and of those who remained in Afghanistan as internal refugees, this population resettled in the safety of the capital city of Kabul. Of only the handful of the Jewish population that remains to this day, the majority of this small populace that fled as refugees have yet to return to Afghanistan.[8] After the Soviets pulled out of Afghanistan in 1989, many of the nearly six million refuges repatriated to Afghanistan, only to face more instability and turmoil in the form of the Taliban regime, economic disparity, food shortages, inflation, and severe drought throughout the coming years. Since Afghanistan is primarily agricultural and rural based, many of those Afghanis raised in refugee camps lack the essential farming expertise needed to survive.[9]

Afghanistan has one of the most poverty-stricken and poorest populations in the world, with the majority of the people living on less than US$2 a day, which is approximately 200 afghanis, the form of currency used in the country. The recent civil war after the Soviet invasion and resulting political instability has delayed the much-needed rebuilding of the country and restructuring of the economy. Children as well as adults face starvation and little to no medical care, and as a result of this, Afghanistan has the highest infant mortality rate in the world.[10] In addition to these dismal circumstances, young orphans struggle for survival and consistently are forced to beg for food and clothes on the streets. Furthermore, because of the overwhelming land mines that litter the land, malevolent remnants from constant warfare, many children and adults have lost limbs by uncovering some of the estimated 10 million mines that remain buried in Afghanistan.[11] As an even further injustice, often those wounded are unable to receive the proper medical care because of a lack of medical facilities.

GOVERNMENT STRUCTURE

Until the middle of the 20th century, the people of Afghanistan lived under the absolute power of the king. After enduring three Anglo-Afghan wars, Afghanistan won its independence from British control on August 19, 1919, a day that is now celebrated as their Independence Day. The Constitutions of 1923 and 1931 upheld the previous rule by monarchy, but the Constitution of 1964 established the new government as a constitutional monarchy with an elected parliament. This differed from the previous rule of an absolute monarch, and the new structure was similar to the U.S. government and included the three branches of the legislative, the executive, and the judicial. This democratic rule was ended by a military coup in 1973 that abolished the 1964 Constitution and established the government as the Republic of Afghanistan. However, political coups and transformations would continue throughout the following decades, including through the period of the Russian invasion and also the Taliban seizure of the Islamic State of Afghanistan, which on doing so in 1996, the Taliban renamed the country the Islamic Emirate of Afghanistan. In December 2001, the Taliban regime crumbled under the coalition led by the United States. Through another episode of political turmoil, the country was returned to a democratic state. As such, Afghanistan's recent political and democratic structure is one of disorder but is beginning to stabilize under the new regime. The current political structure, an Islamic republic, notably arose after the defeat of the Taliban in November 2001. The first democratically held elections occurred in October 2004, and the people elected the country's current president, Hamid Karzai. The National Assembly elections were held in 2005, and the assembly was inaugurated in December 2005. President Karzai and the Afghani government seek to bring stability and optimism back into the lives of the Afghani people.

PROVINCES AND CITIES

Afghanistan is governmentally divided among 34 provinces, referred to as velayat, and these provinces are more commonly recognized as administrative divisions. The major cities in Afghanistan include Kabul, Kandahar, Herat, Mazari Sharif (or Mazar-e-sharif), Baglan, Jalalabad, Kondoz, and Charikar. Kabul is the largest and most populated city in Afghanistan with a population of nearly three million people.[12] Kabul is a central city of economic importance to Afghanistan, and the city's origins date back more than 4,000 years. The city is tactically located between the Asmai and Sherdawaza mountain ranges of the Hindu Kush and also strategically positioned alongside the Kabul River. For as long as there have been wars in Afghanistan, civilizations have fought to gain control of Kabul because of its strategic location along the trade routes to Central Asia. Kabul has often served as the capital for many conquering empires and most notably was made the capital of the Moghal dynasty by Babur in the early 16th century. In 1738, the Iranian conqueror Nadir Shah captured the city and overthrew the Moghal Empire. When Nadir Shah was assassinated in 1747, Ahmad Shah Durrani assumed the throne and continued to expand the country's borders, and through his actions he is credited in history as the Father of Afghanistan. However, it would be in 1776 when Ahmad Shah's son, Timur Shah Durrani, would inherit the throne and move the center of Afghanistan from Kandahar to establish Kabul as the official capital. Today, Kabul has an established business center and experiences continued urban development. In an effort to rebuild the struggling economy, President Karzai supported an effort to open a US$25-million-dollar Coca-Cola bottling plant in Kabul in September 2006. In addition to President Karzai's efforts to increase local and foreign investment in Afghanistan, the government is working toward building an economy that is independent of Afghanistan's illegal drug trade. The plant is part of President Karzai and the Afghan government's plan to rebuild the economy and symbolically show that the government is making strides toward economic growth.

Kandahar is the second-largest city in Afghanistan and is also the capital of the Kandahar province. Kandahar is considered to be one of the wealthiest provinces in Afghanistan and is a major trade center for livestock, silk, and fruit from the region. As part of the historical origins of the city, researchers speculate that this area possibly was established as a farming village approximately 7,000 years ago. The area gained importance when Alexander the Great invaded the region in 330 B.C.E. and established the city of Kandahar. Like Kabul, Kandahar was also fought over by conquering empires because of the city's imperative strategic location along the trade routes to Central Asia. Kandahar served as the capital of Afghanistan under Ahmad Shah Durrani in 1748, but after 30 years the capital would be moved to Kabul.

Located in western Afghanistan, Herat is the third-largest city in Afghanistan with a population of nearly 300,000. The origin and exact dates of the city remain largely unknown, but in ancient times this region was referred to as Aria and was situated strategically along the Central Asian trade routes. As a city, Aria was invaded and conquered countless times throughout history by various empires. Alexander the Great recognized the strategic importance of this area and erected a large citadel in Aria in the fourth century B.C.E. The citadel would be destroyed and rebuilt on throughout future invasions, but Alexander's original foundation remains standing in Afghanistan. As is true throughout Afghanistan and other countries, the Mongolian emperor Genghis Khan famously destroyed this region in the early 13th century. After being rebuilt during the 15th and 16th centuries, Herat was the center for Persian art and architecture.[13] During the Afghani civil war, the city was part of annexation in 1824 and ruled under one of three independent regions of Afghanistan but was restored in 1863 as part of the country of Afghanistan.

Mazari Sharif, also known as Mazar-e-sharif, is the largest northern city and the fourth-largest populated city in Afghanistan. The literal translation of the city means Holy Grave, and it is known throughout the Islamic world as the site of the Blue Mosque, claimed to be tomb of Hazrat Ali, fourth caliph (religious leader) of Islam and the son-in-law of the Prophet Muhammad. The mosque is roughly rectangular in shape, and the center tomb chamber of Ali is one of Afghanistan's greatest treasures. The Blue Mosque also contains the tombs of various Afghan rulers and religious leaders through the centuries.

Afghanistan still has far to go in becoming a stable country. The region has been ravaged, plundered, and devastated for centuries by social unrest and civil warfare. As the country progresses toward rebuilding its infrastructure, the Afghani people still face many challenges and threats. These hardened people have placed their hopes in the newly democratically elected President Karzai with the hope Afghanistan will finally rest from invasion and be recognized as a fundamental country in the world.

NOTES

1. Peter Marsden, *The Taliban: War, Religion and the New Order in Afghanistan*. The two areas of Jalalabad and Helmand are acknowledged regions for opium production, and it is estimated Helmand supplies one-fourth of the world's opium.

2. For additional information on least developed countries recognized by the United Nations, see http://www.un.org/special-rep/ohrlls/ldc/list.htm.

3. Larry Goodson, *Afghanistan's Endless War: State Failure, Regional Politics, and the Rise of the Taliban*. Other countries interested in the political, economic, and social developments of Afghanistan include India, Uzbekistan, Tajikistan, Saudi Arabia, and Turkey.

4. Martin Ewans, *Afghanistan: A Short History of Its People and Politics*. The author disagrees with the comment that the Russians used chemical weapons during the Soviet invasion from 1979 to 1988. Rather, the author claims this was an exaggerated American allegation, most likely to garner support for the mujahideen, the Islamic freedom forces that were trying to defeat the Russians.

5. Malcolm Russel and Ray Cleaveland, *The Middle East and South Asia: Afghanistan*. For more information on the history of poppy cultivation, see http://www.pbs.org/wgbh/pages/frontline/shows/heroin/etc/history.html.

6. As of 2005, population estimates from the United Nations state that the populace totals in Afghanistan were nearly 30 million. See http://www.un.org/special-rep/ohrlls/ldc/statistics.htm.

7. Hafizullah Emadi, *Cultures and Customs of Afghanistan*.

8. N. C. Aizenman, "Afghan Jew Becomes Country's One and Only," *Washington Post*, January 27, 2005. The article credits Zablon Simintov as the last

living Afghan Jew in the country. However, a census has not been conducted and this cannot be confirmed with certainty.

9. Goodson, *Afghanistan's Endless War.* More than six million Afghani refugees fled to Pakistan and Iran, and this exodus is one of the largest recorded episodes in history.

10. John Woodward, ed., *Afghanistan: Opposing Viewpoints.* As referenced and presumably current as of the publication date of 2006, the country experiences 163.07 deaths per 1,000 live births. Further, the average life expectancy is only 42.9 years for the citizen of Afghanistan.

11. Robert D. Kaplan, "Afghanistan Postmortem." During the war with the Soviets, the Russian government and the Communist Party in Afghanistan planted an estimated 30 million land mines throughout Afghanistan. To this day, the majority of these mines remain active and unmarked.

12. Sources include the *World Gazetteer,* "Afghanistan: Largest Cities and Towns and Statistics of Their Population," http://www.world-gazetteer.com, and World Urbanization Prospects, 2005. Other sources include Population Division of the Department of Economic and Social Affairs of the United Nations Secretariat, *World Population Prospects: The 2004 Revision* and *World Urbanization Prospects: The 2005 Revision,* http://esa.un.org/unup.

13. As referenced in the *CIA World Factbook, 2007.*

2

Prehistory: The Emergence of Civilization in Ancient Afghanistan

The dawn of history of modern Afghanistan may be evaluated in the context of how initial inhabitants interacted with the culture, environment, and trade of neighboring regions. When exploring the history of Afghanistan, the region of the Middle East is used as a reference point for determining the origins of the country. In this regard, the prehistory of the Middle East includes the modern countries of Iraq, Iran, and Afghanistan.[1] During the prehistoric period, the term *Mesopotamia* refers to the overall current region of Iraq, while Persia encompassed the region of present-day Iran. While nomadic families advanced and early settlements began to emerge in Afghanistan, the expansion of these civilizations forced the need for trade and exchange with other societies. As such, the region of Afghanistan is evaluated in relation to early trade and interaction with the regions of Mesopotamia and Persia.

The chronology and documentation of the major events in Afghanistan's early history is highly intermittent during these ancient civilization periods. Disappointingly, because of the constant warfare and strife that has plagued this land since the first inhabitation, the prospect of uncovering precious new archaeological finds is often not feasible. To this extent, the damage from war in Afghanistan suggests that extraordinary excavations are regrettably left to the remote chance of archaeologists and anthropologists discovering unearthed prehistoric artifacts. As a result, those discovered artifacts are fiercely protected, even to the extent that the historical treasures located in the History Museum in Kabul were hidden during the Taliban regime so that these pieces would not be destroyed.[2]

PALEOLITHIC ERA: 2,500,000–10,000 YEARS AGO

Often referred to as the Old Stone Age, the Paleolithic era is regarded as the phase and the time when human evolution and civilizations began to flourish and advance. The Paleolithic era is considered to be the most extensive segment of humankind's history and covers a span of approximately 2,500,000 years. On the geologic time scale from a historical and chronological perspective, this period in history is regarded as part of the Pleistocene epoch, which is the period from approximately 1,800,000 to 11,500 years ago. The name *Pleistocene* is derived from the Greek words *pleistos,* "most," and *kainos,* "new." In archaeology, the end of the Pleistocene epoch occurs in conformity with the end of the Paleolithic age.

The period of the Paleolithic era covers the first era of human development and settlement around the world. During this era in early Afghanistan, humans lived in caves or settled on the steppe plains. These primitive settlers lived under harsh conditions, as Mother Nature and the surrounding elements could often be unfalteringly brutal. Surviving in this environment required these hardened steppe people to live in appalling poverty and forced them to fight for food, even with other family members. The crude living conditions of these early Afghan cultures depended on both the ability to hunt and the ability to gather edible plants from the surrounding environment. This era was in the premature stage for humans to build sophisticated weapons and tools, and northern Afghanistan was a prime area for modern *Homo sapiens* to develop and mature physically. As these early humans developed and progressed, they also contributed to the improvement and advancement of Stone Age tools.

LOWER PALEOLITHIC PERIOD: 2,500,000–120,000 YEARS AGO

The Paleolithic period is divided into three consecutive divisions, referred to as the Lower, Middle, and Upper Paleolithic periods. The Lower Paleolithic period is the earliest division of this age in history and the longest, as it covers the time span of slightly more than two million years. The primary distinguishable characteristic of the Paleolithic period—and continually the most controversial—depicts the process of the evolution of the human species. As part of the evolution process, the period began with the introduction of the first stone tools by such hominids as *Homo habilis.* These early humans came into existence around two million years ago and lasted until the introduction of agriculture approximately 10,000 years ago. Furthermore, Paleolithic cultures are determined by the type and assortment of tools dated to their respective time period. These tools have evident characteristics and are able to provide the basis for a system of classification and usually are based on both the type of materials used and the toolmaking techniques themselves.

During the Lower Paleolithic period, the agricultural and farming lifestyle began in the Middle East and thus lessened the need for the traditional hunting-and-gathering method of living, although these methods were still important. Continual evolution and development occurred over thousands of years, allowing humans to advance from a common ancestor to the modern version of *Homo sapiens.* Archaeological finds indicate that early humans in Afghanistan lived in caves or near riverbanks, as stone tools and implements have been discovered indicating that such settlements existed.[3] The Lower period and the first partition of the Paleolithic era is regarded as "the age of stone tools" since during this time period the ancestors of modern humans made ancient stone tools, such as simple axes or choppers. These most primitive tools were constructed from eoliths, which are sizable fragments and pieces of chipped flint and crude stones. These broken stones were fashioned into tools and used not only for cutting and hunting but also as defense. The early hunters and food gathers commonly used the stone tools as handheld axes, which were created by chipping the stone to form a cutting edge or assembled from fragments struck off a stone.[4] As the era progressed, the sophistication and design of these tools advanced as well.

In general, the Late Paleolithic people were known primarily as hunters and food gatherers. The tool kits of these early natives were extensive and included such objects as knives, scrapers, needles, and spears. These discovered artifacts represent the engineering and technological skills of these Paleolithic people and reveal how these tools were made from chipped stone and flint. Discoveries indicating the Paleolithic people's use of wood, clay, and animal parts were vital in the advancement of their civilization. Some of these tools found in excavation sites date back more than 100,000 years, and these types of implements are the first Lower Paleolithic stone tools to be discovered in Afghanistan.[5] These extraordinary findings indicate how Afghanistan played a major role in the formation and development of the early societies in the world.

MIDDLE PALEOLITHIC PERIOD: 100,000–30,000 YEARS AGO

The time frame use to delineate the Lower Paleolithic period from the Middle era is not definitive, and the genesis of the Middle Paleolithic period varies between 300,000 and 100,000 years ago. However, the principal distinction is the Middle Paleolithic period encompasses many *Mousterian* discoveries that suggest an early form of humans lived between 100,000 and 40,000 years ago known as the *Neanderthal man. Mousterian* is a term used by archaeologists to indicate a style of mainly flint tools that are associated with early humans from the Middle Paleolithic period. In this regard, some archaeological finds of this nature indicate that early civilization might have occurred in the Hindu Kush mountain region as early as 50,000 B.C.E.[6] If this proves true, a discovery like this would indicate that northern Afghanistan was among the earliest locations to domesticate plants and animals.

During the Middle Paleolithic period, Neanderthal man was a species that inhabited mainly Europe and parts of western Asia. As part of the evolution of the human species, this controversial subject suggests that the Neanderthal man evolved from *Homo erectus.* Neanderthal remains are often found in caves, and many of these discoveries indicate that these early humans were advanced enough in intelligence to use fire. Furthermore, Neanderthals were known as hunters of prehistoric mammals and enlisted the aid of primitive stone tools. These stone tools are part of the flake tradition, indicating that the Neanderthal man had the cognizant mind and the ability to cut the stones to create a sharper point. In addition, bone implements such as needles were used, indicating that crudely sewn furs and skins were assembled and used as body coverings.

While it is feasible that Paleolithic humans roamed Afghanistan as far back as 100,000 years, credence must be given to actual historical findings, which thus far have been difficult to make in Afghanistan. The cave areas of the country are extensive, and the narrow passageways and caverns into these mountainous areas are seemingly infinite. Since this region of the earth is prone to earthquakes (it is estimated that up to 50 earthquakes occur in Afghanistan each year), this makes excavations and discoveries increasingly complicated and archaeological finds next to impossible. However, the first true findings of life in Afghanistan are the settlements that existed during the Upper Paleolithic period.

UPPER PALEOLITHIC PERIOD: 40,000–11,000 YEARS AGO

In the Upper Paleolithic period, the Neanderthal man fades away to be interchanged by a variety of *Homo sapiens,* including *Cro-Magnon man* and *Grimaldi man.* As part of this era, an amazing number of human cultures, such as the Aurignacian, Gravettian, Perigordian, Solutrean, and Magdalenian, arose and developed in the Old World.[7] This final era of the Paleolithic age marks the beginning of communal hunting and extensive fishing for prehistoric man. The first human-made shelters and primitive dwellings were built, and this also saw the continued emergence of sewn clothing for warmth and protection. Tools were finely crafted and of great variety, including flint and obsidian blades and projectile points. In 1954 in Afghanistan, the cave of Kara Kamar was the first Stone Age site to be excavated, and this is the earliest indication of human occupation in Afghanistan. Excavations and discoveries have uncovered the remains of a human skull that scientists date to be from roughly 30,000 years ago. These skull fragments were found in a cave in the Badakshan area, which is in the northeastern part of the central highlands, and findings from this archaeological discovery dated tools to approximately 30,000 years ago.[8] Furthermore, these early inhabitants also used such objects as bone, horn, and lapis to make necklaces and other personal ornaments for decoration.

As time passed, the Solutrean people of the Upper Paleolithic era migrated to Europe from the east and ousted many of their Aurignacian predecessors. The Solutrean hunters fashioned extremely fine spearheads and hunted wild horses as their primary game. The Solutrean and remaining Aurignacian cultures were replaced by the Magdalenian, and this culture existed during the final and possibly the most remarkable phase of the Paleolithic period. Throughout this period, unearthed artifacts and dwelling remnants reflect a society made up of whole communities and larger societies of hunters and gatherers. Discoveries of Magdalenian tools denote superior skills and hunting techniques, including the sophisticated engineering of an array of items ranging from small microliths to hunting spears of great length and refinement.

While it is significant that these weapons were highly developed and var-ied, the crowning achievement of the Magdalenian era consisted of the cave paintings and murals that have endured throughout several millennia as the culmination of Paleolithic art. Toward the end of the Paleolithic age, humans produced primitive art by painting cave walls with depictions of everyday life. These scenes typically portray such subjects as the hunt of wild animals, and these images also illustrate human interaction and fertility paintings. While no such discovery has yet been made in the mountains and caves of the Hindu Kush, archaeologists and anthropologists still hope to one day unveil these still hidden treasures of Afghanistan.

MESOLITHIC PERIOD: c. 9000–3000 b.c.e.

The Mesolithic period, also known as the Middle Stone Age, is an interim period in human development that existed between the end of the Paleo-lithic period and the beginning of the Neolithic period. The end of the last glacial period more than 10,000 years ago incorporated both the gradual domestication of plants and animals and the development of settled communities. While Mesolithic cultures would continue in Europe until almost 3000 B.C.E., Neolithic communities developed in the Middle East and Persia between 9000 and 6000 B.C.E. In Afghanistan, archaeological finds reveal that early settlers cultivated such products as wheat and barley between 9,000 and 11,000 years ago.[9]

Evidence of Mesolithic cultures indicates a wide variety of hunting, fishing, and food-gathering techniques. Distinctive humanistic traits of the period are indicated in the hunting and fishing settlements along rivers where both fish and much-needed freshwater were abundant. Microliths, the typical stone implements of the Mesolithic period, are smaller and more delicate than those of the eoliths of the Late Paleolithic period. In addition, during this time, cultures and settlements show advancements in pottery, and the use of the bow developed for hunting. Specifically in the Middle East and the region of Afghanistan, the Natufian culture was dominant during the Mesolithic period. Other cultures include the Badarian and Gerzean in Egypt and the Capsian people in North Africa. The Natufian culture provides the earliest evidence of an evolution from a Mesolithic to a Neolithic way of life.

NEOLITHIC PERIOD: c. 6000–2000 B.C.E.

In archaeology, the term *Neolithic* designates a stage of cultural evolution or technological progress distinguished by the use of stone tools, the existence of settled villages reliant on domesticated plants and animals, and the presence of crafts, such as pottery and weaving. The term *Neolithic* has also been used in anthropology to indicate contemporaneous cultures that reveal independent farming communities. The domestication of plants and animals usually distinguishes Neolithic culture from the previous Paleolithic or Mesolithic hunting, fishing, and food-gathering cultures. The Mesolithic period demonstrates a continual transition from food hunting and collecting to a food-harvesting type of culture. Historians support this viewpoint that pastoralism and farming existed in Afghanistan as early as 6000 B.C.E., and it is possible harvesting settlements existed as far back as 8000 B.C.E.[10]

The Neolithic period is also referred to as the New Stone Age, and the completion of the Neolithic period is manifested by such modernization as the rise of urban civilization, the introduction of metal tools, and the first stages of writing. Archaeologists and anthropologists have identified the earliest known development of Neolithic culture, which occurred in southwestern Asia between 8000 B.C.E. and 6000 B.C.E. Here the domestication of plants and animals was most likely begun by the Mesolithic Natufian peoples, leading to the establishment of settled villages based on the cultivation of wheat and grain and the rearing of such livestock as cattle, sheep, and goats. Around

6000 B.C.E., lapis lazuli was being mined with the use of stone tools in the Badakshan region of Afghanistan for trade with Mesopotamia and India.

Between 6000 and 2000 B.C.E., Neolithic culture spread throughout the world, including into Europe, the Nile valley in Egypt, the Indus valley in India, and the Huang He valley located in northern China. In the fertile Tigris and Euphrates river valleys, the Neolithic culture of the Middle East developed into the urban civilizations of the Bronze Age by 3500 B.C.E. With settlements and civilizations blossoming all over the world, the first true urban dwellings in Afghanistan were established between 3000 and 2000 B.C.E.

NOTES

1. Bernard Lewis, *The Middle East: A Brief History of the Last 2,000 Years.* In addition, Peter Marsden, in *The Taliban: War, Religion and the New Order in Afghanistan,* notes the difficulty in determining if Afghanistan is to be referenced as part of the Middle East or Central Asia. In researching this book, both the history of the Middle East and the history of Central Asia were studied, as it ultimately depends on the author's viewpoint as to which region to categorize the country of Afghanistan in these early civilization periods.

2. Alisa Tang, "1,423 Secured Afghan Artifacts Are Returned to Kabul Museum," March 18, 2007, http://www.signonsandiego.com/uniontrib/20070318/news_1n18afghan.html.

3. For additional information on the early humans of Afghanistan, see http://www.Afghan.net/Afghanistan/prehistory.

4. Archaeologists currently debate whether eoliths were human-made or the result of natural processes of stone. Discoveries and evidence of such early tools may indicate human habitation of ancient areas before the oldest known fossils.

5. See http://www.Afghan.net/Afghanistan/prehistory and Louis Dupree, *Shamshir Ghar: Historic Cave Site in Kandahar Province, Afghanistan.*

6. For additional information on these prehistoric archaeological finds in the early history of Afghanistan, see http://www.afghan-web.com/history/chron/index.html.

7. For more information on these early cultures, readers are encouraged to review works appropriate to this time, such as Michael W. Pitts, *Fairweather Eden: Life Half a Million Years Ago as Revealed by the Excavations at Boxgrove,* which discusses the 10-year excavation wherein a multitude of fossils have been unearthed.

8. In 1954, anthropologist Carlton Coon is credited with excavating the cave of Kara Kamar (near Haibak, Afghanistan) as referenced by Nancy Dupree at http://www.zharov.com/dupree/chapter23.html.

9. Marsden, *The Taliban*. Other research reveals that shepherds raised sheep and goats as well in the Hindu Kush region.

10. Martin Ewans, *Afghanistan: A Short History of Its People and Politics*. Historical evidence widely supports that the region of Afghanistan was inhabited during the Neolithic era, whereas its existence during earlier time periods is widely believed but not yet validated.

3

Early Civilization and the Nomadic People of Afghanistan

ARYAN CIVILIZATION: 2500 B.C.E.–700 B.C.E.

While the exact emergence of civilization in Afghanistan is not definitive, the majority of research indicates that the flux of domestication in the ancient land of the Afghans arose between 2500 to 2000 B.C.E. Historians theorize that it was during this time period that the Aryan tribes of Central Asia began to migrate into the region now known as Afghanistan. The Aryans were a faction of the Indo-European-speaking tribes and are believed to have split the Iranian, Nuristani, and Afghan sects throughout this early civilization period. As the tribes began populating the region, Kabul and other major settlements developed and became established as cities.

The term *nomad* is a commonly used to describe the characteristics of the civilizations that established the first settlements in Afghanistan. In its loosest form, *nomad* generally means "wanderer," but this definition gives the misrepresentation of a person traveling aimlessly throughout the countryside or the desert. Nothing could be further from the truth, as nomads do travel, but they travel with the specific intention to establish new and more lucrative dwellings in another area. As difficult as it might have been, these early Afghan nomads purposely traveled to establish new homes in uncharted territory. In some cases, these nomads sought to inhabit the existing homes of family tribes. Clearly this purposeful drive to leave one settlement for another was a survival tool on the steppe plains of Afghanistan, since a settlement in one location might be acceptable during the summer months, but this same area would be uninhabitable in the harsh winters. In addition, the pastoral nomad who herds his flock of sheep, goats, or cows must also move to new regions to provide unexploited fodder for the livestock. To live a cyclical life of settling and resettling was unfalteringly harsh such as the nomads endured in their ritualistic travel and constant movement. This cyclic relocation system created a disturbing environment, and without question this lifestyle placed a weary burden on these early settlers. Yet this livelihood for survival and endurance led to an aptitude of a harsh, unfaltering, and warrior-like mentality.[1] This fiercely combatant culture, developed in the early dawn of humankind, is still ingrained in the livelihood of the Afghans to this day.

The early humans who settled in the region of Afghanistan seem to have been relatively few in number in comparison to the other, more vast settlements that existed during this time period. The Indus valley civilization is the earliest known "city" way of life, and the Aryans were located mainly on the Indian subcontinent of Pakistan. Consequently, civilization ruins are widespread across the continent, factually supporting the scope and extent of the traveling settlements and civilizations that were established. Because of the wide and expansive settlement of this ancient society, the Indus valley culture is regarded as the most extensive of the world's three earliest civilizations. Other early civilizations include the settlements located in Mesopotamia and Egypt, both of which preceded the Indus civilization but were not nearly as large. During their expansive settlement, the Indus civilization established two large cities, Harappa and Mohenjo-daro (both in Pakistan), and also established a multitude of other locations and dwellings as towns and villages. These two cities were somewhat advanced and substantial in size, with dimension estimates as large as one square mile in breadth and population estimates of approximately 40,000 people.

The Indus civilization likely developed from previous villages by the establishment and implementation of a sophisticated method of irrigating the soil. This method, developed by Mesopotamian predecessors, transformed the region and allowed the Indus civilization to achieve the most efficient agricultural benefit of the fertile Indus River valley, even in times of destructive floods. The crucial characteristic in the formation of these early civilizations was to develop a harvestable and productive food crop to feed and nurture the colony. These more advanced civilizations recognized the importance of crop harvesting to provide food and nourishment, and the abundance of food resulted in healthy citizens and a robust population. As this society settled the land and learned how to harness the earth, this flourishing agricultural civilization would inevitably expand its borders along with the growing number of inhabitants. In doing so, the people worked to increase the size and the number of the villages while also expanding the borders of the Indus people.

Trade with neighboring regions was also pivotal for the Indus civilization and included exchange with the nomadic pioneers in Afghanistan. The Indus people cultivated primarily such grain products as wheat and barley, but historical findings include the earliest discoveries of cotton, which would have been a valuable product in the Indus civilization's trade-dependent economy. The region of Afghanistan, was a land rich in minerals and natural resources, and trade with the nomads of the steppe included mainly barter of such elements as gold, silver, and copper. Lapis lazuli, a stonelike gem that was discovered for mining around 6000 B.C.E., was one of Afghanistan's most valuable natural treasures for trade. This decorative blue-colored stone was highly valued by such royalty as the pharaohs of Egypt, and to this day the finest lapis comes from the northeastern Badakshan region of Afghanistan.

Eventually, the civilization entered a state of decline, possibly because of climatic and environmental changes, and this continual fluctuation caused the civilization to abandon its settlements in search of another, more stable atmosphere. However, as other historians have speculated, it is also plausible that this civilization, which once flourished so well along the banks of the Indus River, ceased to exist for another reason. In this theory, the Indus valley civilization was attacked and destroyed by invaders who virtually eliminated the culture. With the experience of almost total abolition, those few who survived most likely merged with other settlements. In a more probable situation, environmental difficulties, such as harsh flooding, the abundance of improper housing construction, and the increasing population, all negatively impacted the civilization in preparation for defense from attackers. This incident would appear to be congruent with other episodes, such as the earlier Aryan attacks on the Indus region. As with the Indus civilization, the early nomadic settlers in Afghanistan faced similar hardships and constraints from the environment in addition to staving off attacks from invaders.

THE MEDES EMPIRE IN AFGHANISTAN: 700–550 B.C.E.

Around 700 B.C.E, a western Iranian civilization known as the Medes migrated into the region of Afghanistan around 700 B.C.E., conquered feeble settlements, and dominated the land. The Medes are believed to have created the first empire in this region, thus marking the beginning of many empires that would toil to overtake the land of the Afghans. The total duration of the Medes dynasty's reign would last for more than 180 years and began with Deioces as the first Aryan king of the Medes Empire. Deioces played a significant role in the history of the Medes when he united seven of the

Median tribes and became their leader. Deioces ruled from 701 B.C.E. until 665 B.C.E. The Medes were fierce rivals with the Persians and would later be overthrown by this society. Throughout this period, the Medes are also associated with another steppe tribe known as the Scythians, a dominant ethnic group that would eventually overthrow the remaining Medes Empire.

The Medes and the early ancestors of the Pashtun tribe that originated near present-day Kandahar, are believed to have adopted the followings of Zoroaster during this period. These ancestors were primarily pagan but are believed to have adopted Buddhist and Zoroastrian traditions because of other cultural influences. Zoroastrianism would be a prominent religious belief in Afghanistan for centuries until the time of the Arab conquest in A.D. 652, when the followings and teachings of Zoroastrianism were nearly eliminated. Today there is a very small following of the Zoroastrian religion (most notably in India), and in modern times they refer to themselves as the Parsis. It is interesting to note that the Parsis trace their ancestral heritage to the Order of the Magi, the same Magi that are referred to in the Nativity story as the three wise men who present the newborn child Jesus with frankincense, gold, and myrrh.[2] While the religion itself was for the most part lost, Zoroastrianism influenced Judaism and Christianity.

Zoroastrianism is a Middle Eastern religion created by the Iranian prophet Zoroaster, who preached widely in the area now known as Afghanistan. The teachings of Zoroastrianism spread along with the early pagan beliefs and then later Buddhism. Scholars recognize the prophet as a notable historical figure, but his date of origin remains highly unclear, and the debate over the beginning of his life is normally dated between 660 and 630 B.C.E. Other scholars believe that Zoroaster's influence started as early as 1200 B.C.E., and if this were the case, it would make Zoroastrianism one of the earliest religions founded. Despite the debate over the exact date of the prophet's birth, the time of Zoroastrianism was the most influential during the sixth to fifth century B.C.E. As the legend unfolds, Zoroaster was renamed Zarathustra after experiencing a blinding vision in the desert. He began preaching throughout the region, but arguably the most pivotal point in Zarathustra's preaching was when he converted King Vishtaspa. Those who debate the origin of Zarathustra's birth also speculate that the converted King Vishtaspa was not the same as the legendary father of Darius I but rather an earlier ruler of the same name. The earlier King Vishtaspa ruled in present-day eastern Iran and in Bactria of modern Afghanistan. However, despite which King Vishtaspa it was, Zarathustra won over the king and consequently became the court prophet. While the motives for conversion remain speculation, King Vishtaspa widely supported Zoroaster and his teachings.[3] After the conversion of King Vishtaspa, the religion spread quickly in the realm and accordingly spread the beliefs of Zoroaster.

In 553 B.C.E., the King of Persia, known as Cyrus the Great, rebelled against his grandfather Astyages, the King of the Medes, and Cyrus finally defeated his grandfather in 550 B.C.E. After Astyages was captured by his own disgruntled nobles and promptly handed over to the jubilant Cyrus, the Medes were now subjugated to their close kin, the Persians. In the new Persian Empire, they retained a prominent position, and many noble Medes were often employed as officials, governors (known as *satraps*), and generals.

THE RISE OF THE PERSIAN EMPIRE—THE RULE OF THE ACHAEMENID DYNASTY: 550 B.C.E.–330 B.C.E.

The beginning of the Persian Empire in 550 B.C.E. plays an important role in the history of the world. The advancements of the Persians were closely studied and recorded by the Greeks, and these detailed accounts have built a solid foundation for outlining the history of Afghanistan. Current maps of Afghanistan and neighboring territories are vastly different than the maps during Afghanistan's control by the Persians. By the time of the Persian conquest in 550 B.C.E., Afghanistan already existed as a culture and society with settlements that were several thousand years old. Beginning with the rule of Cyrus the Great, the reign of the Persians continued for more than 200 years until the defeat of Darius III as the final ruler of the Persian Empire. In one of the greatest anecdotes in the chronicles of history, Darius III and his army were conquered by Alexander the Great in 331 B.C.E., marking the end of the Persian power in Afghanistan and the rise of the Macedonian rule.

At the time of the rise of the Persian Empire, Afghanistan encompassed several provinces of the Achaemenid Empire. Also referred to as Cyrus II, Cyrus the Great ruled the empire from 590 to 530 B.C.E., and he is regarded as the founder of the Persian Empire. Before his ascension to the throne, he conquered the Medes civilization, united the two Iranian kingdoms, and became the King of Persia in 559 B.C.E. Cyrus worked to constantly expand the borders of his kingdom, successfully gaining advancement into Central Asia, southern Asia, and parts of the Indian border. The first Persian ruler would reign until his death in battle in August 530 B.C.E., when his son Cambyses II would succeed him to the throne. Little is recorded about Cambyses II, but most notably during his reign, Cambyses would be successful in conquering Egypt in 525 B.C.E., a feat Cyrus himself wanted but never was able to achieve before his death.[4]

Following the death of Cambyses in 521 B.C.E., a new ruler arose from a different lineage to become king. The new leader, known as Darius the Great (also as Darius I), inherited the throne in a scandalous manner. As described by two renowned Greek historians of the fifth century B.C.E., Herodotus and Ctesias, these chronological descriptions of the Persian Empire record the detailed historical account of Darius's ascension to the throne. However, another derivative of the story exists from Darius's own description of his life story, which is interwoven with legends and tales of his magnificent rule. Some aspects of the story are questionable and contradict other accounts by the Greek historians Herodotus and Ctesias. The story as relayed by Darius I is told in the Bisitun inscription, a trilanguage script carved into a mountain that describes the conquests of Darius I. As the narrative begins, Darius was born as the son of Hystaspes, the satrap of Parthia. Even during his youth when Cyrus the Great ruled, Darius was suspected of plotting to overtake the throne from the Persian king. After Cyrus's death, Darius served as a member of the royal bodyguard with King Cambyses II. The most significant aspect of the Bisitun inscription is Darius's description of how he ascended the throne, for he was not of the royal bloodline and was an unlikely successor to the throne.

As the story begins and according to the accounts of Darius, Cambyses died by his own hand in March 521 B.C.E. In a saga that seems to be as elaborate as a story created for a movie, Darius declared that Cambyses and his brother Smerdis (also referred to as Bardia), both of whom were the sons of Cyrus the Great, were involved in a brotherly battle over the throne and the resulting kingship of Persia. Allegedly on his deathbed, Cyrus the Great promised Smerdis his fair entitlement to a portion of the kingdom, specifically Smerdis's right to claim the eastern provinces of the Persian Empire. Cambyses II would not allow his brother to attain control of a portion of the kingdom, as this would lessen his share and weaken his authority in the empire. As Darius alleges, before Cambyses set off to conquer Egypt, he secretly ordered his brother Smerdis to be murdered. As part of his logic, Cambyses feared that in his absence and quest for new territory, his brother would lead a rebellion and overtake his throne. To squelch the chance for an insurgence, he issued the order to murder his brother, and shortly thereafter Cambyses departed for Egypt under the belief that his brother was no longer a problem, and therefore his throne was safe from usurpation.

However, an unfathomable situation was waiting for Cambyses on his arrival home. When Cambyses returned from his triumphant clash against the Egyptians, he received the news that his brother Smerdis, the same one he secretly ordered to be killed, was indeed still alive. However, as described by Darius, he alleges that an imposter took Smerdis's name and assumed the throne, and this charlatan was a magian named Gaumata. Hence, Gaumata, under the guise of Smerdis, declared himself the king in 522 B.C.E. and seized the kingdom. As surprising as this may seem, at the time it was actually quite common for rulers to have their identity assumed by an imposter. In a life that did not exist with television networks, the printing press, and global communication, it was easy to pull off this feat without much challenge—save for the task of eliminating the genuine individual. Yet as the ruler was eminently aware, there was always someone in the ranks who was eager to move and replace the leader. Thus, as Darius had presented in his historical accounts as justification for his kingship, it was plausible that this incident occurred as he described.

The ruler Smerdis was recognized throughout Asia, and Cambyses set out to fight against him to win back his kingdom. According to Darius, Cambyses realized his plan was hopeless and killed himself, but not before confessing to Darius about the murder of his brother and elucidating the entire fraudulent story. Under the identity of the brother Smerdis, Gaumata was therefore next in line for the throne and ruled the as the Persian king over the empire for seven months. As the legend states, no one other than Darius had the courage to oppose the new king. Darius, believing he was removing the imposter and fraudulent heir to the throne, marched to the kingdom's capital in October 521 B.C.E. Here at the castle stronghold in Media, Darius and his men seized the faux heir Gaumata, took him as prisoner, and then killed him.[5]

As inscribed in the Bisitun inscription, Darius defended his killing of Gaumata and his own ascension as king that he was restoring the empire to the rightful Achaemenid house. Since the accounts of Cambyses and his brother Smerdis are told through the hands of Darius and there are few other recorded historical testaments, many scholars dispute this account. Historians relate to a more realistic account and believe Darius invented this tale of the magian Gaumata, and the murdered king in Media was undeniably the true son of Cyrus. Further, as both his father and his grandfather were alive at the time of Darius's overtaking the throne, it would be unlikely that Darius was indeed the next in line for the kingship. Nevertheless, after the defeat Smerdis in Media, Darius the Great ascended the throne and governed as the King of Persia. His reign as Darius I would last from 521 to 486 B.C.E., and through his rule he led the empire when it was at its most extensive.

Despite the revolts and questionable methods in which Darius ascended to the title of King of Persia, he is considered to be one of the greatest rulers of the Achaemenid dynasty. The Bisitun inscriptions account for 19 battles and describe how Darius defeated nine rebel leaders, all of whom were vying for his crown. In the midst of rebellions and citizen uprisings over various claims to the throne, Darius's army easily suppressed these uncoordinated and impulsive eruptions. Darius was well known for his genius in battle and administration and also for the construction of great building projects. By 519 B.C.E., Darius had established his authority in the east and restored internal order to the empire. As was the sovereign code of behavior, it was important to constantly strengthen the frontiers of the empire and to expand the boundaries of the realm by gaining more supremacy in battle. The battles waged by Darius included his successful attack of the European Scythians, and he also conquered the civilizations in the Indus valley. But in 513 B.C.E. after attempting to finally subdue the European Scythians, Darius decided to push forth and attempted to fight the Scythians of Asia, an effort that even his brother warned him against. As part of this endeavor, Darius I constructed an engineering achievement in his design to build a bridge over the Bosporus Strait in order to advance through Thrace into Scythia. The Bosporus, also known as the Istanbul Strait, forms the boundary between the European part of Turkey and Asia. Darius wanted to attack the nomadic warriors of the steppe and thus secure the empire's foothold in the northern plains. However, Darius made an incorrect geographic assumption that the Hindu Kush Mountains of Afghanistan were near the Black Sea. Thus, in his lack of knowledge, his expedition was doomed for failure, and furthermore the Scythians proved to be too warrior-like and astute for Darius. As part of the legendary battle techniques of the Scythians, they would draw Darius into their territory and falsely retreat, continuing this artificial dance to draw Darius farther west while exhausting his troops and his supplies. After his army advanced for some weeks into the plains of Ukraine, the army ran out of supplies, and Darius was forced to return to his empire without a victory or territorial advancement.[6] However, regardless of his inability to subdue the Scythians, Darius was successful in expanding the borders created by his predecessors.

In addition to enlarging the territory of the kingdom, Darius was a great statesman, and by far his most effective contribution to the Persian Empire was his ability to rule as an administrator. Through his ideas and institutions of administrative law, he brought to fruition the idea initiated by Cyrus the Great to organize the empire into satraps. Darius also implemented a form of taxes to be paid each province, and trade and commerce were increased as land and sea routes developed. Darius also instigated the use of coins in the kingdom while also establishing a standardized form of weights and measurements. Darius was by far the greatest engineer of the Achaemenid dynasty, and he notably instituted a unique style of Persian architecture. At his capital of Susa, he constructed an *apadana,* a great audience hall and residential palace. The palace inscriptions and carvings depict how Darius brought artisans, materials, and skilled craftsmen from all sections of the empire to build the apadana, and this architectural accomplishment is considered to be one of his signature achievements during his reign.

While Darius achieved success in uniting the realms of his empire, he was also respectful of the religious beliefs and followings of his citizens. He recognized the benefit of acknowledging diverse religions and continued the practice of religious tolerance initiated by Cyrus and Cambyses. Darius's personal inscriptions and accounts of his life seem to indicate that his religious beliefs show the continuous influence of the teachings of Zoroaster. The province Bactriana and the capital at Bactria supposedly were the home of Zoroaster.

This area, located in northern Afghanistan, would eventually become known as Balkh. The Persians were found to be tolerable of the Zoroastrian religion and beliefs, with the underlying policy that it was acceptable as long as the followers remained loyal to the empire by paying taxes and sending their sons to fight in the Persian army.

After the death of Darius I in 486 B.C.E., the Persian Achaemenid dynasty in Afghanistan was governed under Xerxes I, who completed many of the great buildings and projects initiated by his predecessor. Xerxes ruled for 20 years until 465 B.C.E., when Xerxes I was succeeded by Artaxerxes I, who moved the capital of the empire from Persepolis to Babylon. Of significance as king of the empire from 465 to 424 B.C.E., Artaxerxes I established the Persian vernacular as the official language of the government. After his death, his eldest son, Xerxes II, succeeded him to the throne. Xerxes II served the shortest reign as king of the Persians, as his brother assassinated him seven weeks later. However, the satrap of Hyrcania and the illegitimate brother Ochus rebelled against the murdering king and killed him. Ochus assumed the throne as Darius II, and he ruled as the emperor of Persia from 423 to 404 B.C.E., and little is recorded of his reign in the empire, except that he was quite dependent on his wife Parysatis, who was also his half sister. After his death, his eldest son, Artaxeres II, was granted the sole title to the throne and not the younger son Cyrus, despite the pleadings of Parysatis. Even after being named satrap of Lydia, Cyrus continued to fight his brother for the throne for several years and began to build a rebellion throughout the empire. Cyrus and Artaxerxes met in 401 B.C.E. in the Battle of Cunaxa, where Cyrus was killed and hence was no longer a threat to Artaxerxes. After his enthronement, Artaxerxes II was the longest reigning of the Achaemenid kings, and it was during his peaceful 45-year reign that most of the monuments in Afghanistan were constructed.

Conversely, the death of Artaxerxes II marked the beginning of violent rule among the sequential heirs beginning with Artaxerxes III, including many stories of betrayal, poisoning, and ascension to the throne by bloody means. In 338 B.C.E., the same year that Philip of Macedon united the Greek states and paved the way for his son Alexander the Great, Artaxeres III died and was succeeded by Artaxerxes IV. After quickly attaining the throne, Artaxerxes IV was poisoned by Bagoas, a trusted social adviser and eunuch. Bagoas is said to have killed all remaining children and heirs to the throne, except for the youngest son, Arses, whom he made king but then poisoned two years later.

With few options, Bagoas placed Darius III on the throne in 336 B.C.E. When Darius attempted to become independent of the powerful vizier, Bagoas realized it was time to appoint a new and inexperienced king by using the old and reliable tradition of poison. Thus, Bagoas tried to murder Darius as well, but by chance Darius was warned beforehand, and in consequence he forced

Bagoas drink the poison himself. Throughout the mid-fourth century B.C.E., the Persian Empire was beginning to disintegrate, and the control of the outlying regions was in complete disarray. The internal storm that had been brewing for some time finally erupted, and the unstable empire was not prepared for the decisive Battle of Gaugamela in 330 B.C.E. At this crucial battle in history, the Persian Empire would fall to none other than Alexander the Great.

ALEXANDER THE GREAT AND THE RULE OF THE MACEDONIANS—GRECO-BACTRIAN RULE IN AFGHANISTAN: 330 B.C.E.–150 B.C.E.

After the Battle of Gaugamela, the Macedonian ruler Alexander the Great conquered the remaining Persian provinces and began to capture the region of Afghanistan. Alexander ruled as King of Macedonia from 336 to 323 B.C.E., and during his short but impressive reign he achieved such feats as overthrowing the Persian Empire, carrying Macedonian arms to India, and laying the foundation to implement territorial kingdoms. Alexander would be regarded throughout history and time as a hero, a military genius, and a man of legend. During his reign, Alexander was widely admired and respected, and to have served alongside Alexander was enough to propel anyone to greatness and, in a metaphorical sense, to have walked among one of the gods.

In 356 B.C.E., Alexander was born in Macedonia to Philip II and Olympias, who was the daughter of King Neoptolemus of Epirus. From the age of 13 to 16, the philosopher Aristotle taught Alexander and inspired him with an interest in philosophy, medicine, and scientific investigation. A decisive moment in Alexander's life came in 340 B.C.E., when his father Phillip II attacked Byzantium and left young Alexander in charge of Macedonia. These successful strategic battles for Alexander, including other instances such as his defeat of the Thracian people known as the Maedi, his command of the left wing at the Battle of Chaeronea, and his courage in breaking the Sacred Band of Thebes, would lay a solid foundation for his military career. However, his father's divorce from his mother Olympias caused severe strain for Alexander, and after an argument at his father's wedding feast to his new bride, Alexander and his mother angrily fled to Epirus. Phillip and Alexander would one day reunite, but the argument had threatened Alexander's stance as the heir to Phillip's kingdom.

Philip's assassination in 336 B.C.E. was allegedly by the princes of the royal house of Lyncestis, a small kingdom in the valley of the Crna that had been included in Macedonia by King Philip. Alexander, who was much admired and highly praised by the army, succeeded the throne without disagreement. He immediately executed the conspirators of his father's murder along with all possible rivals and those who were opposed to him. From the first moment of his accession to the throne, Alexander was intent on expanding the boundaries of the Macedonian Empire as begun by his father.

In 334 B.C.E. and after visiting Ilium (Troy), Alexander encountered his first enemy force, coming face to face with the Persian army at the Granicus River, located near the Sea of Marmara. The strategy of the Persian military was to attract Alexander across the river to annihilate the young king and his Macedonian troops. From a military history perspective, the style of fighting employed at the time was unique. In the combat formation, the front line of troops would be followed behind by another row of troops so that as the solider at the front of the line fell, another solider moved up from behind to replace those who fell in death or who were severely wounded and could no longer fight. Once the Persian and Macedonian armies began to clash, Alexander's army continued to thrash the Persians and cut through the military procession. The Persian soldiers continued to fall until there were no more replacement troops and finally, the Persian line broke. Alexander's army attained victory by pushing through the broken chain and driving the Persian forces into retreat. The majority of the Greek mercenaries under the rule of Darius III fell into carnage, but 2,000 survivors were sent back to Macedonia in slavery.

In the winter of 334–333 B.C.E., Alexander conquered western Asia Minor and exposed the region to the rule of the Macedonians. Shortly afterwards, Alexander overpowered the hill tribes of Lycia and Pisidia. While there is no question that Alexander was a great military leader, some of his victories were sometimes due to a stroke of luck. In one such instance, Alexander gained a significant advantage following the sudden death of Memnon, the skilled Greek commander of the Persian fleet. This severely hindered the Persian army, as Darius had advanced northward on the eastern side of Mount Amanus. While expertise and guidance on both sides were erroneous, Alexander found Darius drawn up along the Pinarus River. In the battle that followed, Alexander won a decisive victory as the struggle turned into a Persian riot and Darius fled the battlefield, ultimately abandoning his own family in Alexander's hands.

Alexander marched south into Syria and Phoenicia, intending to isolate the Persian fleet from its bases and weaken the fighting forces. Alexander continued to capture city after city, and in one of the conquests he acquired Darius's highly valued war chest. Darius wrote a letter to Alexander offering peace, but Alexander's response required Darius's unconditional surrender to him as the new Lord of Asia. While the seven-month battle of Tyre was in progress, Darius proposed a new offer to Alexander. In his letter, Darius offered to pay a ransom of 10,000 talents for his family, and, in addition, Darius agreed to cede all his lands west of the Euphrates. In a legendary exchange, Alexander's trusted adviser Parmenio urged his king, "I would accept, were I Alexander."

Knowing the offer was inferior and unacceptable, the Macedonian general famously responded, "I would too, were I Parmenio."

The capturing of Tyre in 332 B.C.E. is considered to be one of Alexander's greatest military achievements in which the victory resulted in great bloodshed and the surviving women and children were sold into slavery. After conquering Egypt, completing his control of the eastern Mediterranean coast, Alexander returned to Tyre in the spring of 331 B.C.E. As part of his administrative duties, Alexander appointed a Macedonian satrap for Syria and prepared for his advancement into Mesopotamia. While attempting a clever military maneuver, Alexander crossed northern Mesopotamia toward the Tigris River rather than taking the direct route down the river to Babylon. Despite Alexander's cautious efforts, however, Darius was informed of this maneuver from an advance force, and Darius marched up the Tigris to oppose him. Nevertheless, in the decisive Battle of Gaugamela, Alexander pursued the defeated Persian forces for 35 miles to Arbela. In arguably the most brilliant military maneuver of Alexander's career, Alexander realized how he could defeat the Persian troops, and with his Companion Calvary command he was able to break through the Persian line and make charge straight for Darius's chariot. As part of Alexander's military maneuver, the Companion Calvary was Alexander's elite cavalry and guard, and the cavalry worked as the main offensive support of his army. In a metaphor to describe the style of Greek combat of the time, the Companion Calvary would be used as the hammer while Alexander's phalanx-based infantry would serve as the anvil. The phalanx would work to confine the enemy in place, and the Companion Calvary would move in from behind or from the side to attack the enemy. The implementation of this military maneuver gave Alexander the victory at Gaugamela, which finally resulted in his defeat of Persia and thus opened the gates for his control of Asia.

While it is not clear whether Alexander and Darius faced each other on the battlefield, it is at least certain that once Darius realized his enemy was frighteningly close, Darius retreated to evade the clutches of Alexander. Not afraid of the pursuit and with the taste of victory tantalizingly within his grasp, Alexander continued to chase Darius as he fled the battlefield. Alexander had long sought after Darius, and he knew the importance of capturing the king alive so Darius could remain a figurehead for the conquered Persians and thus keep them in control. However, when Alexander's military council was informed of troubling news with Parmenio and the Greek army, the members urged him to return to the battlefield, where he was more needed. As difficult as it was to cease the chase of his enemy, Alexander reluctantly ended the pursuit of Darius and acknowledged the importance of returning to his troops engaged in combat. Darius narrowly escaped Alexander's clutches, and he exiled himself into Media with his Bactrian cavalry and Greek mercenaries.

The Battle of Gaugamela can legitimately be regarded as the greatest military achievement for Alexander, and the defeat allowed Alexander to subjugate the city of Babylon. While not capturing Darius physically, the defeat of the Persian army propelled Alexander to assume his desired title as the Lord of Asia. As an even more astounding feat at the Battle of Gaugamela, historical records indicate that of Alexander's forces, approximately only 100 men and 100 horses were killed in the battle or consequentially died from exhaustion. Yet for the Persian army, more than 300,000 were slain in the battle, and even more than this amount were taken as prisoners.

Alexander had previously captured Darius's wife and children, not to mention his battle spear and war chest of money, yet Alexander gentlemanly agreed to let Darius's family live unharmed at the capital. Continuing to march across the continent, Alexander ceremonially burned down the legendary palace of Xerxes at Persepolis, convinced it would be a symbolic gesture that the Pan-hellenic war of revenge was at an end. Historians contend, however, that the burning of the palace brought shame to Alexander the next morning when he realized what he had done. The following spring, Alexander marched north into Media and occupied its capital, Ecbatana. The Thessalians and Greek allies were sent home, and Alexander continued his personal war against Darius. Alexander would not relent, and his final defeat of the Persians would be marked by his successful capture of Darius. Furthermore, Alexander feared that additional delay would give imposters the opportunity to state they were Darius, as it was quite common at that time for imposters to pretend they were the genuine ruler and thus cloud his defeat of the true Darius by chasing after charlatans. In his continuation of his quest for Darius, who had retreated into Bactria, by midsummer Alexander set out for the eastern provinces at a high speed. At the same time, Bessus, reigning as the satrap of Bactria and companion to the fleeing Darius, grew frustrated and tired of Darius's inability to fight. Bessus believed that since Darius was unable to remain in control of the throne, he should no longer serve as ruler of the Persian Empire. Bessus was consumed with resentment for their current predicament, and he initiated the revolt in which he and his cohorts killed Darius and chained his dead body to a wagon on the side of the road.[7] In spite of their rivalry, Alexander ordered Darius's body to be buried with due honors in the royal tombs at Persepolis. Turning his anger onto a new enemy, Alexander now vowed to defeat Bessus for robbing him of the pleasure to capture Darius alive.

The death and unofficial defeat of Darius in 330 B.C.E. was significant in the formation of Afghanistan. The defeat of the Persian king was the last obstacle to Alexander's self-desired title as the Great King, and soon after Alexander's Asian coinage titled him the Lord of Asia. Alexander continued his advancement to the Caspian Sea, and in Aria he agreed to let the ruling satraps remain in place. In the location now known as modern Herat of Afghanistan, he established the city of Alexandria of the Arians. During the winter of 330–329 B.C.E., Alexander advanced farther into Afghanistan. Alexander and his army marched up the Afghan valley of the Helmand River and over the mountains past modern Kabul. Here in the country of the Paropamisadae, the great Macedon founded Alexandria by the Caucasus. In continuing the quest for Bessus, the army crossed the mountains of the Hindu Kush and proceeded northward over the Khawak Pass. In spite of the tired army, the food shortages, and the harsh terrain of the "Hindu killer" mountains, Alexander brought his army to Drapsaca in pursuit of Bessus and what remained of the Persian army. As Bessus worked to escape Alexander by moving beyond modern Amu Darya, Alexander marched his army toward the region of Bactra-Zariaspa, known as modern Balkh in Afghanistan. Bessus was counting on allegiance with the satrapies in the regions of Afghanistan along with other principalities to join him in the resistance against Macedonian control. After passing over the Oxus River, Alexander sent his general Ptolemy to track down Bessus, who at this point was removed from power by the Sogdian Spitamenes. Bessus was captured, flogged, and sent to Bactra to accept his fate for his crimes, for which the Persian method of punishment at the time was to cut off the nose and ears of the offender. After Bessus received this Persian punishment, he was publicly executed at Ecbatana.

With Bessus now captured, punished, and executed, Alexander continued his quest to defeat the remaining Persian Empire, and accordingly he turned his forces to concentrate on the defeat of Oxyartes, the companion of Bessus and reigning satrap of Bactria. In 327 B.C.E., Alexander still had one province of the Persian Empire to defeat, located in Balkh of Bactria in Afghanistan. In fear of the wrath of Alexander, Oxyartes secured his wife and his daughter Roxana in the fortress of Sogdian Rock, a fortress that allegedly could only be captured by "men with wings." Alexander arrived at the fortress and requested the surrender of Oxyartes and consequently the remaining Persian Empire. With no response from the king, Alexander scoured his troops for volunteers to climb the steep walls of the fortress. On his capture of the fortress of Sogdian Rock, Alexander gazed on Roxana for the first time, a woman whose beauty, legend has it, overwhelmed him. Completely taken with her, Alexander made the daughter of Oxyartes his bride, and the marriage was also an attempt to subdue the Bactrian satraps rule to Alexander. After the wedding, Alexander moved forward with conquering India the then known "far end of the world." In 327 B.C.E., Alexander left Bactria with a revitalized army and marched forward into the world's end. Alexander's dream of completing his empire could not happen fast enough as he sought to march his army to the last corner of India. After again crossing the treacherous terrain of the Hindu Kush Mountains, Alexander thought it best to divide his forces. In performing what he considered to be a maneuvering advantage, the great general sent a portion of his army through the Khyber Pass in Afghanistan, and Alexander led the remaining troops through the hills to the north. Alexander did not have much knowledge of India's vastness beyond the Hyphasis, but the young Macedon was fervent to discover the extent of his soon-to-be-completed empire. The army faced many difficulties after the tiring and exhausting march to the Hyphasis, and eventually the troops were weak from hunger and exhaustion, and these fatigued souls refused to go any farther. Alexander was overcome with anger, but his troops pleaded with him to return home. Finding the army adamant in their stance and the exhaustion and death tolls rising, Alexander agreed to cease the exploration and turn back into Afghanistan. While returning through the Mulla Pass, Quetta, and Kandahar into the Helmand valley of Afghanistan, the extensive attempt at advancement into India took a severe toll on the army, and as such Alexander's march to the world's end proved disastrous. The barren desert, lack of water, and shortage of food caused great distress to his troops, and as a result many of Alexander's followers perished.

Despite not achieving much victory in India, Alexander continued to battle and to expand his empire. After conquering region after region and subjugating different races along the way, Alexander believed that unification of the races would be necessary to successfully amalgamate the empire. Thus, Alexander began his plans for racial fusion after conquering Susa in 324 B.C.E. Alexander celebrated the seizure of the Persian Empire by instituting his custom of combining the Macedonians and Persians into one master race. Alexander believed that uniting the races would make the Persians on equal terms not only in the Greek army but also as satraps of the provinces. In supporting this challenging endeavor, Alexander encouraged his Macedonian officers to take Persian wives, as he himself had married the Persian Roxana.[8] This policy was harshly begrudged by the Greeks and as a consequence brought increasing friction to Alexander's relations with his Macedonians. His determination to incorporate Persians on equal terms with the Macedonians in both the army and the administration of the provinces was severely resented. Macedonians interpreted this as a threat to their own privileged position, especially after many Persian youths received a Macedonian military training. As a further insult to the Macedonian warriors, Persian nobles had been accepted into the royal cavalry bodyguard.

Alexander was widely respected, and history would award him the title of the greatest military general of all time. Alexander's energetic personality, strong determination, and ability to push for excellence with both himself and his army earned him respect and admiration. However, Alexander's plans for racial synthesis were a complete failure since the Macedonians rejected the concept of cultural synthesis, and the customs of the Greeks would remain dominant. Alexander successfully maintained loyalty throughout his reign, and it was only in his unsuccessful attempt to conquer India that Alexander failed to preserve unfaltering allegiance.

In the summer of 323 B.C.E. in Babylon, Alexander was quite suddenly taken ill after a banquet. Historians debate whether Alexander was poisoned or simply died of a natural illness. Alexander clung to life for 10 days, and on June 13 he died at the age of 33. Alexander had reigned for more than 12 years, and his body was eventually placed in a golden coffin in Alexandria. In spite of Alexander's short reign, he had a profound impact and long-lasting influence on the history of Europe, Asia, and the Middle East.

In Afghanistan, Alexander would create many cities, establish a new political structure, and bring a great deal of Greek influence to the region. Alexander's short-lived empire further attests to the incomparable warrior-like mentality of the early Afghans, for not even the great Alexander was able to fully conquer and control their land. The kingdom was divided after his death and Afghanistan was geographically separated by the Hindu Kush Mountains. The Seleucid Empire reigned the lands to the north if the mountain range while the Mauryan dynasty of India ruled southern Afghanistan.

NOTES

1. Erik Hildinger, *Warriors of the Steppe: A Military History of Central Asia, 500 B.C. to 1700 A.D.* The life of the nomad is exhaustingly difficult, and the author argues that the animals can provide only so much for the nomad, such as food and clothing. The nomad must also depend on agriculture to survive, indicating that these early nomads were forced to interact with settled people through trade or other interactions.

2. Herbert Stroup, *Founders of Living Religions.* See also Karl Meyer, *The Dust of Empire: The Race for Mastery in the Asian Heartland*, p. 55. Although referenced with uncertain dates in regard to the Magi's descent from the Zoroastrians, the origins of the religion commenced approximately during the beginning of the Persian Empire with Cyrus the Great.

3. The Avestra is the sacred text of the religion and is divided into five main books and describes the life of Zoroaster, his preaching, and the beliefs of the religion. Some legends tell the story of King Vishtapa, who accepted Zarathustra's (Zoroaster) ideas about one god that were revolutionary at that time. As the tale is told, Zoroaster healed the king's favorite horse, and the king and his court were so impressed that they made Zoroaster the religious council, and thus his teachings began to flourish throughout the kingdom.

4. Bernard Lewis, *The Middle East: A Brief History of the Last 2,000 Years.* Very little has been written about Cambyses II, save for historians noting his penchant for drunkenness and corruption. The lack of information can possibly be due to his short eight-year rein as ruler of the Persian Empire. Quite

possibly as well, he is also overshadowed by two of the greatest rulers in time, sandwiched between Cyrus the Great (his father) and his predecessor, Darius the Great, who ruled the Persian Empire when it was at its most extensive.

5. The story of Cambyses and the imposter Gaumata is mostly recorded by Darius the Great, and his defeat and killing of the false Smerdis was annually celebrated in Persia by a feast called *Magiophani*, which means "the killing of the magian."

6. Hildinger, *Warriors of the Steppe*. Darius was clearly unsuited to try to oppose the Scythians, nomads who were extremely skilled adversaries and steppe warriors.

7. Stephen Tanner, *Afghanistan: A Military History from Alexander the Great to the Fall of the Taliban*. In addition to Bessus, Darius's murderers include Satibarzanes, the satrap of Aria, and Barsaentes, the satrap of Arachosia. After killing Darius, Bessus assumed the title of Artaxerxes as the Great King, and Alexander welcomed the rivalry of the newly titled great ruler in order to defeat him for killing Darius III.

8. Of those who were already married, some 10,000 of Alexander's soldiers with native wives were given generous dowries as compensation.

4

Afghanistan from the Greek Hellenistic Culture to the Introduction of Islam

At the time of his death, Alexander had conquered much of the known world, but in his rush to do so, he failed to secure an adult heir to the empire he left behind. As the story is told, while Alexander lay dying on his deathbed, his generals asked him to whom did he want to leave his empire. Alexander simply replied, "To the strongest." After the death of Alexander in 323 B.C.E., the demise of the great conqueror marked the beginning of the Hellenistic period in Afghanistan. The term *Hellenistic* is a cultural description that is determined by the spread of Greek influence over non-Greek cultures.[1] The death of their great king left the empire in political disarray and resulted in major conflict among the Diadochi, the name of the trusted and high-powered generals of Alexander's army. The period immediately after Alexander's death is eloquently branded as the Wars of the Diadochi, and indeed a war it was—the generals argued and endured a bitter struggle for succession to Alexander's throne that lasted for more than 40 years. The war began shortly after Alexander's death under the Partition of Babylon, which decreed that the territories were to be ultimately divided among the Diadochi. Further, the territories and the ruling satraps were to reign under the oversight of one of Alexander's greatest and most well regarded generals, Perdiccas.[2]

THE DIVISION OF THE MACEDONIAN EMPIRE: 323–310 B.C.E.

As the struggle began for the ownership of Alexander's throne, Perdiccas assumed the role of regent of the empire, which required that as the regent, Perdiccas was in charge of the administrative duties of the empire. A regent is appointed when the successive ruler is unable to serve on the throne, which is most often due to the appointed ruler still being quite young, absent from the throne, or incapacitated and unable to serve. Thus, while acting as regent, Perdiccas recognized the empire was far too extensive and accordingly should be divided among Alexander's generals. At the Partition of Babylon in 323 B.C.E., Perdiccas directed the agreement between the Diachodi and appointed the selected generals to become the satraps of the various provinces. Also in accordance with the agreement, the Diachodi appointed two kings who would share in the overall rule of the provinces. The Diachodi appointed the first king based on general relation to Alexander, as Philip II of Macedon fathered an illegitimate son named Philip Arrhidaeus, and therefore he was Alexander's illegitimate brother and closest heir to the throne. Philip Arridaeus would become Phillip III of Macedon, and he was appointed as heir to Alexander's kingdom along with Alexander's then unborn son. Roxana would give birth to the second king, Alexander IV, several months after Alexander's death.

While Perdiccas continued to act as regent, the Diadochi fought for supremacy over Alexander's vast empire and eventually challenged the rule of Perdiccas. Ptolemy, the satrap of Egypt, was keenly aware that some of the other governors were thirsty for more power, and armed with this knowledge, Ptolemy led the rebellion to oppose the Perdiccas as regent. Perdiccas fought the rebellion for more than a year but was eventually assassinated by his officers in 321 B.C.E. Ptolemy's revolt and usurpation of Perdiccas led to a new division of the empire known as the Partition of Triparadisus. With the continuing struggle for the throne and no regent to protect the rivalry for it, both kings were ultimately murdered. As the older king, Phillip Arrhidaeus was the greater threat and was eventually assassinated in 317 B.C.E. Alexander's mother Olympias was also vulnerable to attack. Her role had become champion and defender of the young grandson Alexander IV as the one true king, and Olympias was ultimately murdered in 316 B.C.E. After living for several years under the almost completely collapsed empire of Alexander, both Roxana and her son Alexander IV were assassinated in approximately 310 B.C.E.

AFGHANISTAN DIVIDED UNDER SELEUCID AND MAURYAN RULE: 310 B.C.E.–180 B.C.E.

The death of the young King Alexander IV marked the beginning of a fascinating aspect in Afghanistan's history, as this initiated the period in time when the country was ruled under two completely different civilizations. During the regent rebellion with Ptolemy, Alexander's cavalry commander Seleucus I Nicator participated in the insurgence against Perdiccas. After the assassination, Seleucus seized control of Alexander's empire in the east and established himself in Babylon in 312 B.C.E. Thus commenced the Seleucid dynasty, and Seleucus successfully extended his authority through the Bactria province in northern Afghanistan. As it was throughout Alexander's rule, the Greek soldiers and colonists would remain in the Hindu Kush region. The dream of racial infusion as originated with Alexander the Great would continue throughout the Seleucid Empire and become part of Hellenistic culture. Seleucus's sovereignty was extensive throughout the region, and he was ruthless in extending the domain of the realm.

The division of Alexander's empire would continue until 306 B.C.E., when the provinces were broken apart into independent kingdoms. In an effort to gain more power and influence over the region, Seleucus pushed the boundaries of his empire as far as the Indus River in India, and it was here in 305 B.C.E. that the Mauryan dynasty of India engaged in a crucial conflict with the Seleucids. After facing a completely devastating battle and almost utter defeat, Seleucus reached an agreement with Chandragupta Maurya, the king of the Mauryan tribe in India. The Indian Mauryan Empire had settled and laid claim to the northern region of the Indian subcontinent, which also included efforts for the colonization of the southern regions in Afghanistan. As part of the battle negotiations and in exchange for land, Seleucus's power would cease south of the Hindu Kush Mountains. As a result, southern Afghanistan would in turn be allocated as a part of the Mauryan quest for territorial expansion from India. The boundaries of the Mauryan Empire hence began from the area south of the Hindu Kush Mountains, stretching from Kabul to the southern Kandahar region. As part of the settlement for the southern area of Afghanistan, the Mauryans agreeably met the payment demands of the Seleucid dynasty. In exchange for this land west of the Indus, Seleucus demanded a substantial force of 500 elephants to strengthen his army, at the time a significant military asset. However, the agreement included the Seleucid Empire's ceding vast amounts of land, not only the southern part of Afghanistan but also considerable sections of Persia.[3] The treaty also included a matrimonial agreement, known as Epigamia in ancient times, although historical records are not particularly clear on the exact specifications of the marriage arrangement. This conjugal treaty could imply either a dynastic alliance between a Seleucid princess and the Mauryan dynasty or a symbolic unity between the Greeks of the Seleucid Empire and the Indians of the Mauryan dynasty. Despite these other treaty stipulations, Seleucus was easily swayed since he desperately desired the strategic value of gaining a large force of elephants as part of his military fleet. This aspect of the treaty would play a decisive role in the Battle of Ipsus in 301 B.C.E., where Seleucus used his fleet of elephants to gain control over Anatolia and northern Syria, and this force assisted in his expansion efforts for 20 years. However for Chandragupta Maurya, the payment of 500 elephants had little impact on his army, which included a force of more than 9,000 elephants.

Regardless of the loss of the vast quantity of land to the Mauryan dynasty, the Seleucid Empire expanded from the Aegean Sea to Afghanistan and brought together a multitude of races and cultural influences. After trying to expand his empire into Europe, Seleucid was assassinated in 281 B.C.E. by Ptolemy Ceraunus. Following Seleucus's assassination, his son Antiochus I Soter would rule from 281 to 261 B.C.E. As his successor, Antiochus would ultimately fail at expanding the empire, which was already undeniably quite vast. The struggle and tearing apart of Alexander's empire would end nearly 40 years after his death with the division of the empire into four territories. The empire was divided among the Ptolemaic dynasty in Egypt, based at Alexandria; the Seleucid dynasty in Syria and Mesopotamia, based at Antioch; the Antigonid dynasty in Macedon and central Greece; and the Attalid dynasty in Anatolia, based at Pergamum. Both Antiochus I and his son Antiochus II, who governed from 261 to 246 B.C.E., were plagued with major challenges in the west, including repeated wars with Ptolemy II and Celtic invasions of Asia Minor. At the end of the reign of Antiochus II, several provinces would rebel and assert their independence from the ruler, contributing to the rise of the Greco-Bactrian secession in 250 B.C.E.

THE RULE OF THE MAURYAN DYNASTY IN SOUTHERN AFGHANISTAN: 305 B.C.E.–185 B.C.E.

This critical time in the history of Afghanistan reflects how the region lived under two different empires with two completely different cultures and religious beliefs. The occupation and lasting influence of the Mauryan dynasty in southern Afghanistan is impressive despite the short rule of the empire outside India. While the Mauryan rule might be considered one of the briefest occupations in the overall history of Afghanistan, the most influential aspect of the dynasty was the religious inspiration it brought to the country, and it is astounding this religious footprint was solidified in such a short time span. As such, the Mauryans introduced Buddhism to the region during their occupation in southern Afghanistan, and Buddhism would become a religion almost as prominent and influential as Zoroastrianism.

In 262 B.C.E., a figure emerged who would play a pivotal role in shaping the religious beliefs of Afghanistan. As the last major emperor in the Mauryan dynasty of India, Asoka was a vigorous supporter of Buddhism. During his reign (dates vary, but his reign was approximately from 262 to 238 B.C.E.), Asoka promoted the beliefs and teachings of Buddhism throughout

India. After leading a successful but rather bloody conquest at the Kalinga country on the eastern coast in approximately 255 B.C.E., Asoka renounced armed battle and embraced what he referred to as the guiding principles of right life. As described by Asoka, witnessing the suffering and pain the war caused on the defeated Kalinga people consumed him with remorse, and he vowed to abandon the life of the sword. After turning to the influence of Buddhist beliefs and principles, Asoka was determined to live his life according to the dharma principle to value all forms of life. Forsaking his years as a soldier, Asoka toiled for the remainder of his life with the philosophy to work for and serve all humankind.

As a further understanding of the humanity of all people, Asoka also developed a policy of respect and acceptance toward all other religious sects. Asoka granted those believers in other faiths the full freedom to live in accordance with their own religious beliefs and principles, but he consistently strove to request that they also work to increase their own inner worth. While supporting their religious expression and beliefs, he still felt obliged to encourage a livelihood of respecting others' religious values, to acknowledge the good deeds and acts of people, and to withhold criticism of the differing viewpoints of others. In this manner, Asoka's goal was to lead people to follow along his lifetime path of dharma through reasoning with people rather than issuing commands to follow his beliefs.

As a result of Asoka's patronage and encouragement to a belief in Buddhism, the religion spread quickly throughout the Mauryan Empire. After Asoka reached enlightenment after the horrific battle at Kalinga, Buddhism spread from a small religious sect that was once confined to a few locations to a widespread and popular belief. During his reign, the religion spread throughout India and subsequently into southern Afghanistan. For the early Afghans who lived south of the Hindu Kush, this period in history was a time of compassion, tranquility, and humanitarianism.

To make his message known, Asoka held oral proclamations for his teachings and his work. To spread his message, his teachings on the principles and beliefs of his religion were engraved on rock and pillar sites. These bilingual inscriptions, known as the Rock Edicts and Pillar Edicts, contain proclamations regarding Asoka's personal thoughts, actions, and life teachings. Two of these Rock Edicts can be found in the southern region of Kandahar and also in Laghman, located in eastern Afghanistan. Significantly, scholars note the tone of sincerity in Asoka's principles and statements, as these writings appear to be his genuine beliefs, and thus it is with positive assertion that Asoka governed his attitude and lifestyle by the dharma values of humanity. Asoka's writings, as inscribed on the edicts, display his authentic passion for charity, compassion, and serving humanity. Furthermore, the Kandahar Edicts are the farthest-western edicts to be found outside India, and the edicts in Afghanistan are the only ones to have used the Greek language. The edicts serve as a remarkable illustration of Afghanistan's role in uniting eastern and western empires and are a perfect representation of the Greek and Indian influence in Afghanistan.

The rule of the Mauryans would decline after Asoka's death, as his death was followed by the rule of several ineffective kings. By the time of the reign of the last Mauryan ruler, Brhadrata, the dynasty and the kingdom had shrunk considerably in size from Asoka's rule. During the Sunga coup of 185 B.C.E., the leader Pusyamitra Sunga assassinated Brhadrata and established the Sunga Empire. By overthrowing the dynasty, the Sunga Empire instituted the beliefs of Hinduism and virtually eliminated the followings of Buddhism, even to the point of threatening Buddhists with persecution. Although historians debate if the Sunga coup eliminated Buddhism in Afghanistan, the Sunga Empire encouraged the beliefs of Hinduism, which became the prominent religion in Afghanistan.[4]

INDEPENDENT RULE IN AFGHANISTAN: GRECO-BACTRIAN AND PARTHIAN SECESSION FROM THE SELEUCID EMPIRE: 250 B.C.E.–125 B.C.E.

The Hellenistic successor states of the Seleucids and the Greco-Bactrians were composed of both Greek and Near Eastern cultures. During this short period in the history of Afghanistan, an independent Hellenistic state was declared in the Bactria region. In 250 B.C.E., Diodotus would declare independence from the empire and assume control of the Bactria province of Afghanistan. By asserting independence, Diodotus formed the Greco-Bactrian kingdom and eventually overthrew the Seleucids and Mauryans in both western and southern Afghanistan. In addition to the Greco-Bactrian revolt for independence, the Iranian rule of the Parthians declared independence from the Seleucids as well. The Parthians established control over the Sistan border region located between eastern Iran and southern Afghanistan. In addition, the Parthians also assumed control of the Kandahar region in southern Afghanistan.

In the northern region, Afghanistan was still under the rule of the remaining Seleucid Empire. The region prospered but was not nearly as peaceful as the southern region under the influence of Asoka. In the northern terrain of Afghanistan, Antiochus III (also known as Antiochus the Great) was the Seleucid king of the Hellenistic Syrian Empire from 223 to 187 B.C.E. During his reign, Antiochus III rebuilt the empire in the east but failed in overpowering the Roman superiority in Europe and in Asia Minor. In addition, during his reign, Antiochus III transformed the empire by reducing the size of the provinces and thus administratively reducing the power of the governing satraps.

As part of his reformation, Antiochus III also believed in the custom of enhancing interaction with neighboring regions by marrying off his daughters to the princes of nearby empires.

Antiochus III pursued his eastward expansion campaign and sought to advance the empire into India from 212 to 205 B.C.E. Antiochus III achieved victory in the northern region of Bactria and defeated the ruler Euthydemus in 208 B.C.E. As part of the defeat, Antiochus decided to allow Euthydemus to continue his reign in title, thus allowing him to serve as a political figurehead.[5] Continuing his eastern campaign, in 206 B.C.E., Antiochus marched toward Kabul by crossing the steep hills and valleys of the Hindu Kush Mountains. Once his eastern campaign was completed, Antiochus III believed that his triumphs entitled him to a higher designation, and thus he assumed the title of the Great King. By taking this name, Antiochus was in one manner paying tribute to the ancient Archamenid title but also encouraging the Greek comparison to Alexander the Great. Antiochus changed his appellation, and accordingly he became known as Antiochus the Great.[6] However, Antiochus would not be honored with this title for very long.

The Seleucid Empire suffered a threefold loss to the Roman Republic at the Battle of Thermopylae in 191 B.C.E., the Battle of Magnesia in 190 B.C.E., and also the sequential defeat of the Seleucid navy. At the Treaty of Apamea in 188 B.C.E., Antiochus the Great agreed to relinquish his control of all his empire in Europe and his landholdings in Asia Minor. Also as part of the massive settlement, Antiochus was forced to submit to the Roman Empire in multiple forms. This included such stipulations as the payment of reparations for the war, which included approximately 15,000 talents paid out over 12 years to recover the costs of the war, and the surrender of his massive military fleet, including his elephants. As further insult, the peace treaty required Antiochus to hand over prisoners, including his son Antiochus IV.[7] The treaty greatly reduced the size of his kingdom to the areas of Syria, Mesopotamia, and western Iran, but in return the Senate granted him a Roman agreement of peace and friendship. However, the agreement of these embarrassing stipulations would still not result in amicability between the empires. In three years' time, Antiochus the Great would be murdered in a temple near Susa, a city located in present-day Iran. After seizing control, the Greco-Bactrian rule spread quickly over multiple territories and by 170 B.C.E. reached from northeastern Iran in the west to the Ganges River in India. However, internal disputes between the Greek and Hellenized rulers inundated the empire and weakened the strength of the kingdom. Further, the exceedingly ambitious attempts at conquering and extending the boundaries of the empire farther east in India contributed to the demise of the dynasty.

In 180 B.C.E., Demetrius I of Bactria invaded India and formed the Greco-Indian kingdom, which in consequence ended the Mauryan dynasty. This

kingdom would rule in Afghanistan's Bactria region until 125 B.C.E., when the
empire was invaded and overthrown by nomadic tribes from the north. The
empire was overrun by two groups of northern nomadic invaders from Central Asia, believed to be the Parthians of eastern Iran and the Sakas; historical
accounts also allege that the invading nomadic tribes possibly included the
Scythians. In approximately 135 B.C.E., a loose confederation of five Central
Asian nomadic tribes united together under the one Kushan tribe, and this
newly unified tribe banded together to fight and conquered the Afghan area.[8]
During their conquests, these nomadic invaders established control over Sistan (the border region between Iran and Afghanistan) and Kandahar in the
south, previously controlled by the Parthians.

THE KUSHAN EMPIRE: 150 B.C.E.–A.D. 224

The Yuezhi people conquered Bactria in the second century B.C.E. and divided the country into five chiefdoms, one of which would become the Kushan
Empire. Recognizing the importance of unification, these five tribes combined
under the one dominate Kushan tribe, and the primary rulers descended from
the Yuezhi. As an integrated people, the Kushan overtook the land from the
Bactrian Greeks and ruled over most of the northern Indian subcontinent, Afghanistan, and parts of Central Asia. The rule of the Kushan Empire would
endure for nearly four centuries and would cross over into the Christian era
of history. The domain of the empire spread from the Kabul River valley of
the Hindu Kush into Asia as far as the central Indian plateau. Under King
Kanishka I, who reigned from A.D. 78 to 144, the Kushan kingdom was recognized along with China, Rome, and Parthia as one of the four great Eurasian
powers of the time. King Kanishka was by far the most powerful ruler of the
Kushan Empire, and during his reign the empire reached its greatest breadth,
stretching from Afghanistan into Asia and including the locations of Kashmir
and Tibet.

As patrons of religion, the Kushan Empire was instrumental in spreading
Buddhism throughout Central Asia and China, and King Kanishka particularly encouraged Asoka's beliefs of Mauryan Buddhism. As part of the Kushan
Empire's penchant for religion and art, the world's largest Buddha figures
were carved into a cliff in the Bamian (Bamyan) Mountains of Afghanistan.
The two statues, each measuring approximately 175 feet and 120 feet tall,
were an iconic tribute to the religious beliefs of the enlightened one. Commonly referred to as the Buddhas at Bamian, the statues were located along the
ancient trade route in the Bamian valley, approximately 143 miles northwest
of Kabul.[9] The statues were widely regarded as a perfect representation of
Greco-Buddhist art and influence to the region of Afghanistan but regrettably
were destroyed as part of the Taliban regime in 2001.

Under King Kanishka, the Kushan Empire became affluent through trade, particularly with the Roman Empire. However, in addition to trade with the Romans, the Kushan carried luxury goods and traded with vast empires such as India and China via the Silk Road at Balkh in Afghanistan. As part of their successful ability and affinity for trade, the Kushan gold coins exhibit the figures of Greek, Roman, Iranian, Hindu, and Buddhist deities and furthermore displayed Greek letters and inscriptions. These images and inscriptions on the coins demonstrate the influence and magnitude of the various forms of religion and art that prevailed in the Kushan Empire. After achieving this zenith of religious and cultural acceptance, the Kushan dynasty would never be as powerful as it was under King Kanishka. In the third century A.D., the empire was segmented into several smaller kingdoms. Several Kushan princes governed in various kingdoms throughout the empire, but this weakened the empire and thus left the kingdoms vulnerable to attack. After the Kushan Empire separated into several kingdoms, the trade interaction with China and Rome simultaneously decreased, and in consequence this severely impacted Kushan prosperity. With no unity in the kingdom and no income to assist in the kingdom's defense, the Sassanian Empire of Persia easily overtook the control of Afghanistan from the Kushan Empire. After the rise of the Sassanian dynasty in Iran and of the local powers of the Gupta dynasty in northern India, the Kushan rule declined and ultimately ceased. As a result, the Sassanian kingdom established control over parts of Afghanistan in approximately A.D. 241.

CONTINUOUS CONQUEST—THE SASSANIAN DYNASTY AND WHITE HUN INVASION: A.D. 241–565

The Sassanian dynasty would rule in Afghanistan for more than a century, but the dynasty still was not able to unite and fully conquer the region. As a result, northern nomadic invaders easily defeated the Sassanian dynasty in A.D. 400. Afghanistan was yet again invaded by another group of conquerors, this time the fierce Hepthalites of Central Asia. The Hepthalites were also referred to as the White Huns, and these ferocious attackers swept into Bactria and into southern Afghanistan, obliterating any remaining Kushan and Sassanian kingdoms along the way. The White Huns also engaged in continuous conflict with the western Sassanians. The rule of the White Huns lasted for nearly 200 years in Afghanistan, and during this time the country was ravaged and destroyed by these Indo-European nomadic invaders.[10]

The Western Turks overthrew the Hepthalites in the mid-sixth century A.D. The Western Turks were also nomads of Central Asia, and in the conquest in A.D. 565, the Hepthalites lost control of their territories north of the Amu Darya. The concurrent resurrection of Sassanian control forced the Hepthalites to also relinquish control of the lands south of the Amu Darya. Afghanistan was subsequently ruled under several small kingdoms, the majority of which were ultimately under Sassanian rule led by either Kushan or Hepthalite monarchs. Impressive archaeological findings of this time period indicate humans lived in the caves of the Hindu Kush Mountains, and historians speculate that people sought refuge in these caves while the Hepthalites and the Sassanians battled for supremacy in Afghanistan.[11] As a result of the severe impact of the Hepthalites in this region, some historians speculate the name Afghanistan is derived from Faganish, the name of the fierce Hepthalite king who declared this region as the land of Fagan. Since the Hepthalites engaged in constant warfare with neighboring tribes for nearly 100 years, the incessant conflict severely strained the internal strength of the White Huns. By the mid sixth century, a sect of the Western Turks known as the Gokturks had defeated the Hepthalites in the territories north of the Amu Darya, and the Sassanians had defeated the last of the White Huns in the lands to the south.

Along with the Sassanian rule also came the renewed influence of Hinduism in Afghanistan. The exact date of the emergence of Hinduism is shrouded in obscurity, but civilizations in mid-seventh-century Afghanistan constructed Hindu kingdoms in the areas of Kabul, Gardez, and Ghazni. Historical findings of marble statues of Hindu deities, including the elephant god Ganesh, have been discovered in the cities Ghazni and Koh Daman.[12] Other remnants discovered include the carvings of the Hindu goddess Shiva and her consort Durga. The exciting discovery of these Hindu treasures represent a remarkable facet in Afghanistan's history, and these statues currently reside at the country's National Museum in Kabul.

THE RULE OF ISLAMIC EMPIRES IN AFGHANISTAN

During the pre-Islamic period in Afghanistan, the cultural religious beliefs functioned mainly under the threefold influence of Hellenistic, Buddhist, and Hindu cultures. China and Rome also had influence on the region as indicated in the artesian artifacts found in Afghanistan. The year A.D. 642 marked the beginning of the Arab conquest of the Middle East. In this year at the Battle of Nahavand, Islamic warriors overpowered the Sassanian Empire. For 10 years, the Arabian Empire defeated and overthrew the remaining Parthinian and Byzantine empires. By A.D. 652, the Arabs had invaded and conquered Afghanistan, and thus began the emergence of the Islamic faith in Afghanistan. There is a clear distinction made in that while the conquest and the emergence of Islam do run in tandem, it was not the intent of the Arabs to introduce Islam by force. The Arab Empire conquered the remainder of Afghanistan from A.D. 706 to 709, and over time the majority of the population converted to Islam.[13] As the culture and influence of Islam spread, Afghanistan emerged as the center of several dominant Islamic rulers.

For several centuries in Afghanistan, the country became the focal point for many distinguished empires, most notably the Ghaznavid Empire that reigned from A.D. 962 to 1151. Certainly of unique origins, the Ghaznavid Empire began when a slave guard (referred to as a *malmuk*) of the Turkish Empire, revolted against the ruling Samanids. Alptigin was a Turkish malmuk from Ghazni, and he established the Ghaznavid Empire by usurping the throne of the weakened Samanid Empire. As has often been the case throughout history, the rights to the throne lay in the usurper's personal strength and the determination to overthrow those in power, and Alptigin crossed the Hindu Kush Mountains from Balkh with this intention and sequestered Ghanzi from the declining Samanid Empire. Mainly a Sunni Muslim establishment located on the eastern side of Afghanistan, the fort was located advantageously on the Silk Road between Kabul and Kandahar. After seizing control of the Fort of Ghanzi in A.D. 962, the once-insignificant settlement was transformed into one of the most dazzling capitals of the Islamic world.

The center of the Ghanzi Empire was the pinnacle of prestige, enjoying artisans, poets, musicians, and philosophers amidst the backdrop of opulent palaces, gold-encrusted mosques, and abundant gardens that spread to India. Throughout the reign of the empire, many iconoclastic movements were unleashed into India, and the empire spread from Afghanistan into India, Persia, and Central Asia. After the Battle of Dandanaqan in A.D. 1039 with the Seljuks, who were another Muslim dynasty of Turkish descent, the Ghaznavid Empire lost control of the western territories, including the western part of Afghanistan. The Ghaznavids were forced to rule while being presided over by the Seljuks of Iran, and the empire never returned to the same opulence and splendor.

Historically, the Ghaznavid Empire is significant because it was the first considerable Islamic empire that spread across Asia. At the empire's greatest extent, the domain of the Ghaznavid Empire was vast and encompassed much of modern Iran, Afghanistan, India, and Pakistan. Of further historical significance, the Ghaznavids are believed to have spread Islam into India, a land that was dominated by Hinduism. For the next century, the Ghaznavids' diminished rule was still extensive until the Ghorid Empire would overthrow the remaining territories in A.D. 1151.

The last Ghaznavid king of the empire, known as Sultan Bahram Shah, engaged in antagonism and opposition with the Ghori Empire. Founded by Muhammad Ghori, his descendants ruled over a diminishing empire that was consumed with bitter struggles and competition. King Ala'uddin Ghori conquered Ghazni in A.D. 1151 while trying to quench his anger over the death of his brother, and as revenge he set the city ablaze for seven days. The Ghorid Empire would reign in Afghanistan from A.D. 1151 to 1219 and would continue the lavishness that began under Ghanzi rule. At the height of the empire, the boundaries extended from modern Iraq through Afghanistan and as far to the east as India. The region flourished with wealth and opulence, speckled with lavish palaces surrounded by magnificent gardens. In this land of the Afghans, the soil thrived from the remarkably engineered irrigation systems that led water to fields and gardens of splendor. In A.D. 1219, the empire and the land of Afghanistan would be ransacked and overthrown by a ferocious Mongol warrior the likes of which the world had never seen.

NOTES

1. The term *Hellenistic* is accredited to German historian Johann Gustav Droysen.

2. Stephen Tanner, *Afghanistan: A Military History from Alexander the Great to the Fall of the Taliban.*

3. Colin Mason, *A Short History of Asia: Stone Age to 2000 A.D.* The impact of Seleculus's agreement to cede vast amounts of land is something that historians continue to debate. Even though he relinquished control of these lands, Seleculus's victory at Ipsus was due solely to the elephant brigade he acquired under this treaty. Nevertheless, historians still debate if the exchange of land for elephants was the best choice for the Seleucid Empire.

4. Authors such as Romila Thapar in *Asoka and the Decline of the Mauryas* debate the end of Buddhism in Afghanistan.

5. This method is also in accordance with the code of Alexander the Great, as Alexander wanted to capture Darius III alive because he recognized the political significance of retaining the ruler to serve as a figurehead, which would stifle a rebellion from the conquered empire.

6. Antiochus III's title of "The Great" was briefly assumed after his Eastern Campaign and appears in historical accounts through 202 B.C.E. After his victory at Koile Syria, Antiochos assumed the Greek title "Basileus Megas," Greek for "Great King."

7. In the comprehensive treaty, the terms of the hostages were very clearly stipulated. This entailed the selection of 20 hostages by the Roman council, and these hostages would be traded out every three years.

8. Historical evidence and excavations in Ai Khanoum indicate the invasion by nomadic cultures. Located in the Kunduz region of northeastern Afghanistan, the site was excavated between 1964 and 1978 but was abandoned at the beginning of Afghanistan's war with the Soviets. Afterward, very little original archaeological evidence remained because of damage from the war or thieves raiding the site.

9. The majestic Buddhas at Bamyan were destroyed by the Taliban in 2001, and several countries, such as Japan and Switzerland, have pledged support for the artistic rebuilding of the statues.

10. The White Huns are also well known for their ruthless destruction of Buddhist shrines in Afghanistan.

11. Louis Dupree, *Shamshir Ghar: Historic Cave Site in Kandahar Province, Afghanistan.*

12. These remarkable findings lead scholars to conclude that the Hindu God Ganesh actually originated in Afghanistan.

13. Bernard Lewis, *The Middle East: A Brief History of the Last 2,000 Years,* p. 57. Lewis notes the difference in the emergence of Islam and that it was spread not by conquest but as a gradual change in society.

5

The Mongolian Invasion
through the Shah Dynasty

The Mongols demolished Central Asia by conquering cities and leaving a trail of devastation in their wake. To this day in Afghanistan and Pakistan, descendants of the Mongols still exist and include the ethic groups of the Mongol, Hazara, and Aimak peoples. The very name *Mongols* literally translates as "the invincible ones," and this translation certainly describes the attitude of these ruthless invaders in the 13th century. The name *Mongols* originally referred to one of the smaller warlike tribes in Central Asia, and in A.D. 1206, the noble warrior Temujin united this trivial tribe with the other prominent ethnic groups. As a result, *Mongols* ultimately referred to the overall collection of the tribes that marched across Central Asia, and thus the term eventually resulted in the all-encompassing Mongol Empire.

Born to a noble chieftain, the story of Temujin's birth depicts a gallant prophecy for his life as a Mongol warrior. As the mysterious shaman forecasted, Temujin entered the world with enormous strength in his hands and proclaimed that one day Temujin would become a significant force in the world.[1] Temujin's life began well, but these early years did not last for long and ended abruptly when Temujin's noble father was murdered out of tribal rivalry. This swift fall from grace forced Temujin and his family into exile, and for many years their only option for survival was to seek refuge in the nearby mountains and forests. Throughout these years of refuge, Temujin and his family lived in banishment among the forest trees, and the harvesting of plants and berries in addition to hunting marmots and rats for food provided their only sustenance. This experience resulted in Temujin's mentality of becoming toughened, cold, and bitter to the surrounding world. As further evidence of the ruthless lifestyle he endured throughout his early years, Temujin even killed his own brother as the result of an argument over stealing food. After merging back into tribal society, Temujin married his first wife, Borte, around the age of 16. However both were captured by a local Merkit tribe soon after the marriage. Temujin escaped and later returned for his wife, assisting her escape under the cover of darkness. During her capture, Borte was supposedly forced into marriage with a Merkit chieftain and nine months later, Borte gave birth to her first child. The issue of paternity clearly plagued Temujin and as a result he named his son Jorchi, the Mongolian word for "visitor" or "guest."

Temujin's mother played a pivotal and guiding role in his life not only by teaching him how to survive in such a harsh landscape but also by instructing him on the need for forging alliances as a strength against opponents. Practicing these early life lessons, Temujin quickly conquered disparate tribes as a fierce Mongolian warrior and quickly gained recognition throughout the Mongolian community. Eventually, Temujin cleverly ascertained the magnitude of merging the tribe of the Central Asian confederations under one inclusive tribe, the result of which would fuse the Mongols into a more resilient force. By the time Temujin unified the tribes, he was already nearly 60 years old. Part of his reason for the unification was Temujin's desire for revenge against the Jurchen, a neighboring tribe that had often instilled conflict between the different Central Asian tribes. The Jurchen were also known also for seemingly unjustly executing the Mongolian people, and Temujin could no longer tolerate such excessive oppression.

The unification of the tribes distressed local empires since some of the critical trade routes were now part of the territory of the "invincible ones." As rightfully feared, these empires were concerned that the much-needed items for commerce would be confiscated along the trade route and placed under the control of the Mongols. As such, the Mongol alliance was a severe threat to the neighboring regions—and clearly not without justification. However, these tribes should have worried more about Temujin's birth-prophecy, and the trepidation to come. On a dark night in 1206, in a dimly lit sanctuary set aglow by burning candles and smoldering cinders, the Mongolian assembly of tribal chiefs declared Temujin the "universal ruler," the translation of his new title of Genghis Khan.

MONGOL RULE IN AFGHANISTAN: 1219–1332

After overcoming some difficulties at first, Genghis Khan mercilessly defeated and conquered the well-protected cities of neighboring empires. By

1209, the dreaded Genghis Khan was acknowledged by the Tangut emperor as the reigning lord of this region. Genghis Khan continued to annihilate the various dynasties until these empires were under his domain. Less than 10 years later, by 1218, the Mongol Empire was extensive and spread from the Caspian Sea to the Persian Gulf.[2]

Genghis Khan worked to unite his power with neighboring empires and sent communication to the Khwarizm Empire in Afghanistan, conveying his message that he was the sovereign ruler of these lands. As such, he presented an amicable letter of friendship and in accordance requested the Khwarizm ruler to accept this declaration of Mongolian supremacy. The letter was accompanied with treasures and vast wealth, including such riches as gold, silver, silk, furs, and a flock of 500 camels. The caravan never reached the shah and instead was seized by an overly greedy border commander who was overcome with the prospect of all the wealth and fortune in the caravan. The commander killed all the convoy members save one, a camel boy who escaped unnoticed and returned to Genghis Khan to tell him of the incident. Furious, Genghis Khan dispatched a messenger party to the shah and ordered him to immediately agree to the previously delineated terms, bow to the Mongolian army, and deliver the border commander for punishment. The overly confident Shah naively refused such a declamation, and as further insult he killed the sole Muslim messenger and sent the other Mongol couriers back to Genghis Khan with shaved beards.[3] This offense might have stifled any other potential invader, but the act was too insulting to Genghis Khan. Whether or not he intended to destroy the empire before the gesture of amity, the Shah's response sealed the kingdom's fate. Ruthlessly and unfalteringly, the Mongol ruler unleashed more than 200,000 Mongol soldiers into Afghanistan, crippling cities such as Herat, Balkh, Ghazni, and Bamiyan and slaughtering every man, woman, and child along the way.

The Mongols conquered and destroyed the Khwarizm Empire from 1219 to 1221, and afterward Genghis Khan divided the army into two separate forces. He led his army on a forceful storm across Afghanistan, Pakistan, and India, destroying the region as punishment for the shah's insulting actions. His other military force, led by his two top generals, Jebe and Subutai, marched their soldiers through Russia and the Caucasus. For the most part, the campaign was not to ruthlessly kill and destroy, but rather to subdue those in these lands by pillaging settlements and forcing the inhabitants to recognize Genghis Khan as the only universal ruler of the world. After several years of adding more territories to the empire, including Persia, the once-divided forces united again in Mongolia in 1225. Genghis Khan was callous in his avenging defeat of these lands, and historical records describe vast fields filled with the skeletal remains of slain enemies and slaughtered horse carcasses scattered among the bodies on the battlefield. The stories of the Mongols' method of conquest were extremely terrifying, for once the army entered the city, bodies and blood filled the streets as punishment for refusing to bow down to the Mongol ruler. When provoked, angered, or extremely insulted, Genghis Khan was brutal in his methods, and in one such instance he poured molten hot silver into the eyes and ears of his enemy as retribution for a previous insult.[4] The legend of these malicious methods caused many shahs to tremble in fear of the Mongol army. Understandably, once this fear was instilled in a man's heart, it was hard to find the courage to fight such savage warriors. For those that would not submit to the Mongol army, the Mongols' ruthless mission was for the most part a simple instruction from Genghis Khan: slay the men, rape the women, and enslave the children.

Genghis Khan instilled advanced military disciplines to his army, including such concepts as psychological warfare, communication intelligence, and advanced mobility tactics that encouraged combat on horseback. The Mongols were highly skilled and unrivaled riders, learning to ride horses beginning at the very young age of three. As a magnificent illustration of the Mongols' equestrian dexterity and control of the three horses with which the rider traveled, the rider was skillful enough to jump from his fatigued horse to a fresh steed in the midst of combat while still being able to continue firing arrows at the enemy. This ability granted the Mongols a significant advantage over their less-equestrian-knowledgeable adversaries and even presented a deceptive impression of the Mongols having more riders than originally estimated on the battlefield.[5] Genghis Khan organized an extremely efficient army composed of strict discipline, tremendous loyalty, and remarkable adeptness. The Mongol army was thus an intense military force that was the most feared and ruthless power to enter the battlefield. By using their highly developed skills in military techniques of surprise, ambush maneuvers, and extreme mobility, the Mongols were able to defeat enemy armies with swift vengeance and merciless punishment. While these shocking actions may be regarded as the acts of menial and inferior savages, the Mongols were anything but inferior in intellect.

As further evidence of his military genius, Genghis Khan used supply routes to create multiple communication stations, known as *yams,* throughout the Mongol Empire that worked to gather and quickly disseminate communication intelligence. The Yam communication network was an ingenious invention, as this system revolutionized and greatly increased the spread of communication and the ability to relay military intelligence throughout the Mongolian Empire. The yam network was specifically designed for the Mongolian messengers, who often covered great distances of nearly 200 kilometers over one or two days, and these messengers arrived at relays stations along the route for food, water, and spare horses.[6] Genghis Khan's desire to understand and defeat his enemy may be considered passionate to the point of being fanatical, and as a result his extensive spy network was unrivaled.

As demonstrated by the Mongols' ability to quickly subdue enemies, the conquering Mongol army was keenly adept at learning the strategies and techniques of the defeated empires. In the Mongols' desire to learn the methods of defeated opponents, they spared only those with certain skills from death, such as engineers and architects. If these skilled opponents agreed to live as slaves to the Mongolian Empire, they would be useful for the expertise they provided as it related to war. As a result of this strategy, the most significant contribution came from the Chinese engineers who taught the Mongols how to strike and defeat walled cities. Of the few enemy soldiers that acknowledged Genghis Khan as the one universal ruler, these soldiers were included as part of the Mongol army. Not only did this technique expand the army, but it also gave the Mongols the advantage of learning new military techniques to use against other enemy forces. Hence, the Mongolian Empire grew not just in domain but also in intellect as the army continued to pillage and devour other empires while learning their secrets along the way.

The Mongols were one of the most ethnically and culturally diverse empires in history, composed of mainly nomadic inhabitants from all regions. Keenly aware of the cultural differences of his empire, Genghis Khan was supportive of the various religions in the empire as long as they did not challenge his rule.[7] As a further testament to the strength of the army, he refused to divide his troops into different ethnic sects. Since he recognized that this would be a weakness and could segregate his army, Genghis Khan believed in supporting a sense of unity and loyalty among the conquered tribes through the integration of all individuals throughout the army despite their cultural differences. Hence, the Mongolian army would fight as a force of one unified people composed of multiple ethnicities rather than as divided units of smaller clans based on religious, tribal, and ethnic backgrounds. Of course, despite the resistance or disagreement, discipline was strictly enforced and included severe punishment for those who tried to oppose his policy.

Genghis Khan imposed a revolutionary concept on the Mongol army by basing his military on the Asian decimal system. The army was divided into units, the most basic of which was composed of 10 men known as an *arban*. In this regard, each man was assigned to his arban for life, and it was forbidden under any circumstance, whether religious, cultural, ethnic, or simply dislike of his other members, to leave and join another group. The leader of the arban then reported to the leader of the *jagun*, the next highest unit composed of 100 soldiers. The remaining units included the *mingghan* (1,000 men) and *tumen* (10,000 men). Both units employed the title of *noyan* for the leader, which indicated a form of respect as a military commander, but noyan was not considered a military rank. To further the seriousness of the strict regime of the army, it was a grave insult and disgrace if a solider chose to abandon his arban. As punishment the entire arban would be executed for this treason. If all 10 men of the arban deserted, then the entire jagun would be executed. The leaders of the tumen were regarded as Mongol nobility, and the title *Khagan* (Great Khan) was the designated term for the leader of 10 tumens, which was reserved for Genghis Khan himself.[8]

As was the typical terrain and climate of Afghanistan, the Mongol warriors were accustomed to the extreme weather conditions. Interestingly, the Mongols preferred to travel during the winter months in order to better navigate across rivers. Further, these hardened nomads were used to traveling great distances in little time. The Mongols often traveled without much difficulty, seeing as they were accustomed to these conditions as part of their nomadic lifestyle. Despite working under these harsh circumstances, the Mongols were exceptionally skilled at siege warfare. Such military methods included the diversion of rivers and tributaries to towns and cities so as to weaken the opponent's defenses. In addition, the army would often take enemy prisoners and force them to march in front of the army as a shield when engaging in combat with other enemy forces. By far the most devastating practice—and arguably the most favored technique by the Mongols—was to simulate retreat and feign escape from the battlefield. Once the enemy army was lured into a faux victory, the pursuit of the seemingly retreating Mongols would break up the enemy army into smaller sections, and the Mongols would skillfully lure them into an ambush. As is often the case in history, Genghis Khan was blessed with a cadre of extremely gifted generals who were exceptionally skilled for the time they lived. In having such an elite general force as the tumen commanders, their keenness for military maneuvers allowed Genghis Khan and the Mongols to excel and crush his opponents.[9]

After a conquest, the Mongol army would plunder the villages, and the valuables stolen after such defeats were the only payment the soldiers received. Those who resisted were killed. The massacre totals in the region of Afghanistan are particularly startling in Herat, Nishapur, and Samarkand. In one legendary tale of the Mongols' fierceness, an Afghan woman was captured and cleverly tried to beg for her life by arguing that she had swallowed a pearl and that it would be wise not to kill her with the precious treasure in her belly. Swiftly, without hesitation, and while she was still breathing, her stomach was sliced open as the soldier rummaged through her entrails for the tiny orb. On hearing the account, Genghis Khan instructed the soldiers to search all bodies in the same manner, and each inhabitant was turned inside out so that their bowels could be searched for other concealed treasures.

In the early days of August 1227, the great Khan was plotting to overthrow the Hsi-Hsia (Xi Xia) dynasty near the Liupan Mountains when he was suddenly struck ill. He ordered his closest commanders to secretly carry him to the nearby forest in a covered cart, and in this manner he could continue to outline the final defeat of the Hsi-Hsia dynasty away from spying eyes.

Genghis Khan knew that the Hsi-Hsia army would have a decided advantage if they realized he was dead, and thus he was carried away in secret so that the severity of the illness would not be leaked. His closest advisers carried him off with the grim hope that the healing plants of the forest would help him recover. On August 18, 1227, Genghis Khan succumbed to the mysterious illness, and the great leader was dead. While living a rather ruthless life, he requested that his death not be known, and he ordered that he be buried without any markings.[10] There are several legends regarding the death of Genghis Khan. These tales include orders that were so secretive that the grave site was to be trampled with horses or even buried under a river that was diverted over his grave. As legend has it, the burial party was to be killed by another party and then that one as well so that the grave site would never be discovered. Whatever legends have unfolded to obscure the circumstances surrounding the true death of Genghis Khan, historians agree that the burial was so enigmatic that the tomb and final resting place remains undiscovered to this day.

History has often presented Genghis Khan in a negative view, with the majority of observers citing his destructive and cruel nature. The Mongolians regard Genghis Khan as a cherished and revered ruler and believe historical records are inaccurately harsh and embellished.[11] Embracing the positive attributes of Genghis Khan, he instituted valuable practices gained from his knowledge and ability to master others' trade crafts. He instituted several unique practices, such as tax exemption for religious leaders, doctors, and some teachers. He introduced many liberal regimes while embracing artistic and cultural growth. His extensive yam communication and checkpoint network was unequaled in his time, and his efforts at increasing communication resulted in his development of a written language for the Mongols. By leading the Mongols in capturing the Silk Road, he bought control to the trade regions and allowed increased communications between the Middle East and Central Asia. His enforcement of traditional Mongolian beliefs and traditions provided stability for the Mongolian Empire, and for this he is celebrated as a hero in Mongolia.

Yet, despite these benefits, Genghis is widely known for the destruction he brought to many countries. In Afghanistan, he is remembered as a detrimental and genocidal ruler who ransacked and pillaged the land. His purposeful drive to destroy the irrigation systems in Afghanistan left the region an unfertile desert of sand, and the ramifications of his actions are still felt to this day. Because of his spitefulness for revenge and penchant for burning vast amounts of land, Genghis Khan is blamed for the barren and unfertile soil in Afghanistan. Through his conquering and invading army, Genghis destroyed the cities of Herat, Balkh, and Ghazni; plundered the once-fertile agricultural soil; and slaughtered countless Afghan civilizations.

At the time of his death in 1227, Genghis Khan's Mongolian Empire was vast but not as extensive as it would become after his death. Genghis Khan designated that his empire would be shared among his four sons, Ogedei, Chagadai, Tolui, and Jochi. Before his death, Genghis Khan contemplated the difficult decision of which son would inherit his empire, and he eventually discussed the situation publicly with all four of his children. He was concerned that the oldest son, Jochi, might have been fathered by a Merkit when Jochi's mother Borte was held captive. To the statement that the empire would go to the oldest, the second son, Chagadai, burst out that he would not be subjugated to live under the rule of a bastard child. After agreeing that they both would work together in the empire, Chagadai purportedly suggested the empire be bequeathed to the third son, Ogedei, as he was the most deserving. Genghis agreed, and the empire was bestowed to Ogedei, but despite his designation as the successive Khagan, all four of Genghis's sons would receive a portion of the empire.[12] The empire was divided into Kanates, which were designated as subterritories, and their ruling Khans were to follow the one great Khan Ogedei. This included the rule of the Kipchak Khanate in present-day Russia, the Chagatai Khanate in western Asia, the Ilkhanate in Persia and the Middle East, and the Great Khanate ruled over Mongolia and China.

Women were regarded as important in the Mongolian Empire not only in terms of family life but also to serve in leadership positions. As the men fought on the battlefield, the women were imperative to the success of the empire by remaining on the home front to administer and manage the empire. After Genghis's death, his third son, Ogedei, ruled the one part of the empire but was never in a coherent state to rule because of his penchant for drunkenness. Ogedei's wife ruled for more than 10 years, serving as the administrator of the empire. Her efforts were widely recognized, and her influence as queen was even acknowledged on the seal of the empire.[13] During Ogedei's reign, the expansion of the empire would be significant, and his nephew Halagu Khan reigned while defeating the Muslim lands to the southwest, including the modern countries of Iran, Iraq, Afghanistan, and Pakistan. The rule of the Mongols in Afghanistan would continue under the Ilkhanates and was advanced under the domination of Timur Lang.

RULE OF THE TIMURID EMPIRE: 1370–1506

In the late 14th century, a man by the Turkic name of Timur arose as the new great leader of the Mongols and also as the founder of the Timurid Empire in Central Asia. Before his rule, he was regarded as a fugitive and hid in the mountains of Afghanistan for protection. During his time in exile, he engaged in combat with other expelled rebel warriors. It was either during this rebel carousing or in an attempt to steal a sheep that Timur was injured, and the damage would change his name. As a result of this situation, his knee was pierced by an arrow, causing him to limp and thus earning him the name Timur Lang, or Timur the Lame.

As a bloodline descendant of Genghis Khan, in 1369 Timur returned to the center of the Kart Empire at Balkh to claim his kingship. Timur overpowered Amir Husayn, the fellow fugitive turned noble aristocrat who once forged a strong alliance with Timur. After his capture and execution, Timur seized Amir Husayn's vast empire centered in Balkh, and rather than assuming the title of shah, he desired to be called the *amir*, the Turkic word for prince or nobility.[14] Until his death 35 years later, Timur would subject the land to endless wars and bloodshed, much like Genghis Khan had during his reign. However, unlike his ancestor Genghis Khan, Timur is credited with rebuilding the cities he destroyed. Timur believed that once a city was claimed as his own, despite being razed to the ground, it should be rebuilt to display the glory of the Timurid Empire. After defeating part of the Persian Empire in 1383, Timur marched along the Helmand River toward Herat, destroying all the irrigation systems along the way. Once he captured the city of Herat, he ruthlessly massacred all inhabitants. In these instances, Herat and Balkh were destroyed and rebuilt by Timur to embrace the artesian culture and atmosphere Timur desired. The capital city of Herat would flourish and be adorned with beautiful buildings.[15] This embodiment of annihilation continued for the next 20 years, including the invasion and capture of Baghdad in 1401 that killed more than 20,000 residents. Some of Timur's bloody conquests saw the death counts expand to nearly 70,000, yet his time of rule in Afghanistan is regarded as one of peace and prosperity.

On Timur's death in 1405, the time had come yet again for a familiar story, one that had previously occurred in Afghanistan. The fight began among the Timurids over the throne of the empire, and rival family clans erupted to seize their rightful claim to the throne. After many years and bloodshed, Timur's youngest son, Shah Rukh, would emerge as the heir to the kingdom, which stretched from China to the Tigris River in Iraq. Shah Rukh governed from the capital of Herat, and, much like his father, he was a passionate supporter of the arts and cultures of the region. The kingdom celebrated artisans, philosophers, and poets the likes of which had not been seen since the Kushan rule in the third century. To this day in Herat, many artifacts and designs from the Timurid Empire are celebrated and embraced for their striking intricacies and inspiration. The hostility for the throne began again in 1447 after Shah Rukh's death and was further amplified after his wife Qawhar Shad was murdered 10 years later. The reign of Sultan Husain Baiqara from 1468 to 1506 would continue the glory of Herat, but unfortunately his kingly duties focused on opulence rather than administration of the empire. He was easily overthrown and removed from the seat of power in Afghanistan, and once more, at the end of the Timurid Empire, the battle for enthronement began in Afghanistan.

MOGHUL AND SAFAVID RULE: 1506–1709

Afghanistan was divided into several sections throughout the 16th, 17th, and 18th centuries. In the early 16th century, a man emerged who would fight feverishly and gallantly for his kingdom, all at the young age of 17. Originally named Zahiruddin Mohammad, he was renamed Babur and was a descendant of Genghis Khan and Timur Lang. Already the ruler of the Kingdom of Ferghana, Babur was the founder of the Moghul Empire and made the capital at Kabul in 1504. Furthering the empire's expansion efforts, in 1522 he seized the city of Kandahar, and he marched into Delhi in 1526. His achievement and victory in India would be a pivotal point for Afghanistan. At the First Battle of Panipat, Babur defeated the last sultan of the Delhi Empire, Ibrahim Lodi after having been informed of an internal schism in the sultan's communication channels. Babur led the attack on India with a force of 12,000 soldiers and easily overthrew the sultan's disconcerted army of 100,000. Under Babur, the Muslim armies, composed of Mongol, Turkic, and Afghan warriors, invaded India.

Afghanistan continued to endure countless expansion conquests throughout the 17th century under two primary empires. The Moghuls of India avidly ruled from Kabul, while the Safavids of Persia ruled from Herat. The Safavids of Persia challenged the Moghul Empire, and the Persians overtook the area in the middle of the 17th century. The expansion conquests would continue into the early 18th century in approximately 1707, increasing Afghanistan's borders from south of the Hindu Kush and the eastern provinces into India. The city of Kandahar was divided among a fierce rivalry between the two most important tribal groups—the Ghilzai and the Abdali tribes—and the Abdali would later be known as the foremost Durrani tribe. As a result of the intense hostility between these tribes, the greater part of the Abdali tribe had previously been transferred to Herat. This gave the Ghilzai more power by residing as the majority tribe in Kandahar, and eventually the Abdalis fostered bitter resentment that intensified into hatred and revenge.

Under the Persian rule at Kandahar, the court at Isfahan began to decline, and the tribes became increasingly impatient. Previously, the court had been tolerant of the differing religions in Afghanistan, as the court was mainly Shi'ite Islam, while the Kandahar tribes were mainly Sunni Muslim. However, a new Sufavid leader named Sultan Husain had decided to put an end to the religious tolerance, and as such he sought to convert all the tribes under one religion. The rivalry between the tribes became overbearing, and the sultan appointed a Georgian noble named Abdullah Khan to cease these insurgences. Under his rule as the new governor of Kandahar, Abdullah Khan was given the arduous task of forcing all inhabitants to convert to Shi'ism. The new governor was defeated by the Baluchs, and in response to these insurgents, the court sent Gurgin Khan to meet with Mirwais Khan Hotak, the influential leader of the Ghilzai. Gurgin Khan was a Georgian man known for his adamant strictness against rebellion, and on arrival and without hesitation, he captured and imprisoned the usurpers. Aware that Mirwais was the mastermind behind such rebellions, Gurgin sent him to the court at Isfahan to be treated as a dangerous criminal. On arriving at the center of the Persian Empire and the nucleus of domination over the Afghan people, Mirwais observed firsthand the accounts of decadence and decay at the court, and this solidified the reports that the Persian Safavid Empire was on the brink of collapse. However, because of Mirwais's wealth, diplomacy, and penchant for persuasion, the Persian sultan shielded Mirwais from punishment, and he was released as prisoner and returned to Kandahar. With the newfound enlightenment of knowing firsthand how the court had grown weak, Mirwais devised plans for ousting the despot Gurgin. If his plans were successful, these tactics would lead the way for ending the Persian control in Afghanistan.[16]

THE FIRST AFGHAN STATE AND TURKMEN RULE: 1709–1747

In 1709, the Pashtun tribesmen under Ghaznavid Khan Nasher revolted against the Persian Safavids. These Afghans moved into power and briefly ruled the region under a sentiment of Afghan independence that was bravely championed by Mirwais Khan. During this heightened sense of autonomy in Afghanistan, Mirwais seized his chance and assassinated Gurgin. Details of the assassination vary, but according to the Kandarian legend, Mirwais invited Gurgin to a picnic on his country estate outside Kandahar. The guests dined on rich food and strong wine until they were consumed with drunken debauchery. In a coordinated attack launched at the most opportune moment, Mirwais struck and killed Gurgin and his escorts, and Mirwais led the rebellion as they marched to the citadel. The court at Isfahan was in no position to battle, as the empire of the Safavid Persians had weakened considerably in corruption and debauchery, while the tribes had become impatient. Mirwais Khan established Kandahar independent of the Safavid Persians through the imprisonment of emissaries and in the defeat of the Persian army. In 1708, the Persian court could do nothing but watch in astonishment as Kandahar was taken from their kingdom. Mirwais knew that if they were to remain free, the tribes would have to be united, and he worked for this until his death in 1715. His brave acts solidified him in history as Afghanistan's first great nationalist, and he was laid to rest in a blue-domed mausoleum at Bagh-i-Kohkran outside Kandahar, near the very orchard where he assassinated Gurgin Khan. After his death, his brother was to assume the throne, but Mirwais's son was thirsty for power. Mir Mahmud killed his uncle and moved to the seat of power, and in 1722 he invaded Persia and occupied the Safavid throne at Isfahan. In 1725, he was mysteriously killed and was succeeded by his cousin Ashraf, who ruled until 1730. By this time, the Afghans began to lose control of Persia, seeing as the unification led by Mirwais never materialized under his successors.

Nadir Shah of Persia pushed back the Afghans in the Battle of Damghan in 1729, and furthermore Nadir Shah marched on Isfahan and defeated Ashraf, removing him from the seat of power. After occupying southwestern Afghanistan for two years, in 1738 Nadir Shah conquered the remaining provinces of Afghanistan, seizing Kandahar and occupying Kabul, Ghazni, and Lahore. The assassination of Nadir Shah in 1747 resulted in a *Loya jirga* (grand council) in which Ahmad Shah was chosen king. After his enthronement in 1747, Ahmad Shah changed his name to Ahmad Durrani, meaning "pearl of pearls" in Persian. The Durrani Empire became the principal Afghan ruler until the British invasion in the early 19th century. The Durrani Empire would establish the government structure that exists in Afghanistan today, but the country's borders would not be defined until the arrival of the British.

NOTES

1. John Man, *Genghis Khan: Life, Death, and Resurrection.* As was customary at the time, a shaman examined the newborn for the sign of an omen. Given the birth name Temujin, the shaman declared that a blood clot on his right hand was a symbol of strength. The date of birth for Temujin is not certain but is believed to be approximately between 1155 and 1162.

2. David Morgan, *The Mongols.* Historical accounts sometime accredit him as Chinggis Khan.

3. For more information on the story of the Mongol invasion of Afghanistan, see http://www.afghanan.net/afghanistan/mongols.htm.

4. Man, *Genghis Khan.* This references the execution of Inalchuq (Inalchuk), Genghis Khan's enemy whom he pursued endlessly for months. The capture of Inalchuk was a dramatic experience that resulted in his imprisonment and brutal public execution.

5. Time-Life Books, *The Mongol Conquests.* The Mongol rider would travel with three horses in order to jump from horse to horse with the least exhaustion. The Mongolian horse was a prized aspect of the Mongol army, and the rider's swift ability often made the army fight as if they were double or triple in numbers. Those horses that served and died in battle with exceptional swiftness and agility would be skinned and preserved as honored vestiges.

6. Morgan, *The Mongols.* As presented by the author, the yam system was more of a communication network for the Mongols to correspond efficiently and swiftly within the massive empire. Marco Polo regarded the yam communication system as an impressive and highly advanced means of transmission, and his own descriptions of the network give more historical accuracy than the Mongols. In addition, the author refers to Genghis Khan by the Mongol spelling Chingiz.

7. Genghis Khan was supportive of all religious beliefs but executed those who resisted the Mongol rule, such as the Ismaili Muslims.

8. The *Secret History of the Mongols* (author unknown and written in 1240) specifically differentiates the meanings behind *Khaghan* and *Khan.* In the Mongol Empire, there were only five true Khagans, which consisted of Genghis Kahn and his direct descendants, including Ogedei, Kublai, Mongke, and Guyuk Khan. The title of *Khaghan* is thus reserved for the emperor of imperial rank and in translation means Khan of Khans, similar to King of Kings. Other rulers are referred to as Khans despite the large amount of rulers who claimed the title Khagan.

9. Stephen Tanner, *Afghanistan: A Military History from Alexander the Great to the Rise and Fall of the Taliban.* As further support to the mystical alignment of the forces, other examples in history include the generals of Alexander the Great—Parmenio, Hephaestion, Craterus, and Perdiccas; the marshals of Napoleon Bonaparte—Massena, Davour, Ney, and Murat; and the generals of Robert E. Lee—Jackson, Longstreet, Stuart, and A. P. Hill. The author argues these leaders, much like Genghis Khan, were successful because of the rare happenstance of the exceptionally talented leaders who surrounded them.

10. Man, *Genghis Khan.* There are several legends regarding the death of Genghis Khan. The author argues against these biblical legends, believing instead that the death was not marked with occasion because of the severe secrecy involved. The entire death of Genghis Khan is omitted from *The Secret History of the Mongols,* the staple reference text of the Mongols written in the 13th century, and notes nothing about the burial. As Jack Weatherford notes in *Genghis Khan and the Making of the Modern World,* it was Mongol tradition to be buried without a monument, as the soul would live in the revered Spirit Banner. Stephen Tanner, on the other hand, in *Afghanistan,* states that Genghis Khan died with his servants and family around him, his death no more glamorous than that of old age (accelerated by a possible fall from his horse). The great Khan was buried in a vast chamber of enormous wealth and opulence and seated on his throne. Other accounts describe that the great Mongolian leader requested to be buried with 40 young virgins and 40 horses to join him in the afterlife.

11. Man, *Genghis Khan.* As part of this negative view, during the harsh siege of Beijing in 1214, the Mongols are said to have engaged in cannibalism dur-

ing the long winter. The author notes that the evidence to support this claim is from non-Mongol sources that prefer to present the negative viewpoint of the Mongols, and thus the statements regarding cannibalism are probably not valid.

12. Weatherford, *Genghis Khan and the Making of the Modern World*. The young Temujin would toil endlessly to regain his wife Borte when both were captured by the Merkid. After dramatically rescuing her, the young couple returned home, and Borte delivered a son that Temujin named Jorchi (which translates to "visitor" or "guest"). The true paternity of Jorchi would haunt Temujin and the royal empire throughout his rule as Genghis Khan, and many referenced Jorchi as the bastard son of the great khan.

13. Weatherford, *Genghis Khan and the Making of the Modern World*.

14. *Amir* or *emir* means "commander" in Arabic. Some historians argue that Timur was not particularly brilliant in political maneuvers and this choice of title was an unwise decision in his attempt for recognition.

15. Justin Marozzi, *Tamerlane: Sword of Islam, Conqueror of the World*.

16. Tanner, *Afghanistan*. The author uses Gorgi as an alternative spelling of Gorgin.

6

The Durrani Empire through the Anglo-Afghan Wars, 1839–1919

During the 19th century, the confrontation between the expanding British and Russian empires for territory in Central Asia drastically impacted Afghanistan. Primarily, the British were concerned with the growing number of Russian forces encroaching into the Central Asian countries, most notably into India and Persia. This increasing aggression and escalating concern resulted in a series of three separate wars in Afghanistan, and this period in history is affectionately referred to as "The Great Game."[1] The heightened rivalry during the Great Game also contributed to the Siege of Herat during 1837–38 and the Panjdeh Incident in 1885. During the Siege of Herat, the Persians tried to retake Afghanistan and drive out the British and Russian occupation, and the city of Herat was severely destroyed during the encounter. During the brief skirmish of the Panjdeh Incident, Russian forces seized territory at Panjdeh in Afghanistan and killed nearly 600 Afghan soldiers. In an effort of British diplomacy, the incident was diverted from a full-scale war by negotiating a settlement with the Russians, but the event would be significant in the launch of the Second Anglo-Afghan War several years later. However, as part of the competition between Russia and Great Britain, the launch of the First Anglo-Afghan war in 1838 is regarded as the first major conflict of the Great Game.

the authoritative agreement, Ahmad Shah Durrani appointed his second son, Timur Shah, to protect the Durrani Empire and ensure order in India while he marched east back into Afghanistan.

However, Ahmad Durrani would not be in Afghanistan for long, as on returning to Kandahar in 1757, he was informed that the Maratha Confederacy in India had swiftly and successfully exiled the court of Timur Shah. Ahmad was forced to return to India and declared a *jihad,* known as an Islamic holy war, against the Maratha's. A multitude of tribes heralded the call of the holy war, which included the various Pashtun tribes, the Balochs, the Tajiks, and also the Muslim population residing in India. Led by Ahmad Durrani, the tribes joined the religious quest and returned to India, easily defeating minor skirmishes along the way. In 1760, the army had reached Lahore and moved forward to face the Maratha army. The Marathas had also banded together into one great army, and this Indian defense vastly outnumbered Ahmad Shah and his forces. With both sides vying for control of northern India, the Third Battle of Panipat was fought between Ahmad Shah's Muslim army and the Hindu army of the Marathas in January 1761. The Muslims had soundly defeated the Hindus, and these circumstances were regarded as the high point of Ahmad Shah's power and control. The Third Battle of Panipat would position the Durrani Empire and Afghanistan to become one of the largest Islamic empires in the world.[4] In spite of this triumphant victory, his peaceful control would soon be plagued with other challenges in the kingdom, and thus remaining at the pinnacle of the empire would not last long for Ahmad Shah.

The domination and control of the empire began to loosen in 1762 when Ahmad Shah Durrani crossed Afghanistan to subdue the Sikhs, followers of an indigenous monotheistic religion of India found in the 16th century by the guru Nanak. The Sikhs were a threat to the Durrani Empire because they had gained considerable control in the Punjab region, and in doing so the Sikhs had become a powerful opponent to the empire. Ahmad Shah greatly desired to subdue the Sikhs, and his army attacked and gained control of the Sikhs's holy city of Amritsar, where he brutally massacred thousands of Sikh followers. Not only did he viciously demolish the sacred temples and buildings, but he ordered these holy places to be covered with cow's blood as an insult and desecration of their religion. All this was in an effort to subjugate the Sikhs permanently, but Ahmad Shah and his successors would not be successful in this endeavor.

Similarly in northern Afghanistan, the Uzbeks rebelled against Ahmad Shah's regime, leading to many consequential revolts in the north. On the recognition of his inability to subdue these insurgents, Ahmad Shah reached a compromise with the Uzbek Emir of Bujhara. The agreement stipulated that the lands to the north of the Amu Darya would remain under the Uzbek's control and that the lands to the south would belong to the Durrani Empire. After many years of combating the Sikhs, Ahmad Shah's health began to decline, and he withdrew to his home in the mountains in 1772. His villa was located to the east of Kandahar and would be where he would spend the remainder of his life.[5] By the time of his death several months later, Ahmad Shah had lost all control of the Punjab region to the Sikhs. The Sikhs would remain in control until being defeated by the British in the First Anglo Sikh War in 1846. In spite of his defeat by the Sikhs and the Uzbeks, Ahmad Shah successfully balanced tribal alliances and unity, his overall goal aimed at diverting rebellion. Ahmad Shah Durrani is credited with unifying these tribes and forging a nation composed of a multitude of ethnicities and cultures. After his death, the Durrani Empire had been established both west and north of Kandahar, and for his efforts in unity and the remarkable role he played in establishing Afghanistan, he is regarded as Ahmad Shah Baba, the "Father of Afghanistan."

RULE OF TIMUR SHAH DURRANI: 1772–1793

Historically, it is not unusual to have a strong and charismatic ruler followed by several weaker and less triumphant successors. Unfortunately, history would once again repeat itself, for after Ahmad Shah's death, the other Durrani rulers would be regarded as incompetent governors of the empire and lose much of the territory that had been acquired under Afghanistan's beloved father. Within 50 years, the Durrani Empire would for the most part no longer exist, and without question the empire certainly never exceeded the zenith once attained by Ahmad Shah. Throughout the duration of the Durrani decline, Afghanistan would be torn apart in multiple Anglo-Afghan civil wars and serve as a territorial tug-of-war between the prominent European powers of the time.

Despite his failure in subjugating India in 1757, Timur Shah was named Ahmad Shah's successor, and several historians consider that this selection was most likely only because he was the king's son. The Durrani chieftains grudgingly accepted Timur's appointment to the throne, still quite leery of Timur's inadequacies in the menial administration of his father's territories in northern India. Timur's reign would last for more than 20 years, from 1772 to 1793, and most of this was spent fighting Afghanistan's civil war and in trying to calm other rebellions in the empire. As a result of these continuous tribal outbreaks and his inability to control them, Timur was forced to relocate the capital from Kandahar to Kabul. As a result of these tribal circumstances, his inadequate response to the events during his reign, and in examination of the overall history of Afghanistan, he is regarded as one of the most incompetent and weakest rulers to govern the country. Historians believe that because of his inability to govern and squelch rebellions, coupled with his overall lack of political savvy and military ability, it was only a matter of time before the Durrani Empire began to unravel under his hands.

ZAMAN SHAH DURRANI: 1793–1801

Interestingly, Timur had a large family that included 26 sons.[6] His fifth son would succeed him to the throne on his death in 1793, but several others would become the sovereign leaders of various territories in the Durrani Empire throughout the remaining decades. Zaman Shah Durrani was the fifth son of Timur, which seems perplexing at first for the fifth son to attain the title of king, as usually the oldest or second oldest inherits the throne. However, at the time of Timur's death, he had not announced a designated heir but instead left a multitude of sons, leading to disorder and chaos over who would succeed him. Zaman held the prestigious title as the Governor of Kabul; however, two of his brothers were also considered the primary contestants for the throne. As such, the other main competitors besides Zaman were his two brothers who governed Herat and Kandahar. While all three served respectful positions as the governors of prestigious cities, Zaman held the upper hand by being the governor of the capital. His ability to vie for the crown was aided by the respectable *wazir* Painda Khan, who had served as the deputy to Ahmad Shah. With these substantial factors pushing him to the forefront of the competition, Zaman became shah at the young age of 23, and his reign as king would last from 1793 to 1801. However, his path to the throne was not for lack of animosity, and many of his brothers were imprisoned in the capital for trying to revolt against the kingdom and elect a new shah.[7] These factors threw Afghanistan into turmoil, weakening the country internally and thus making the country more susceptible to attack from foreign countries.

Meanwhile, other European powers were continuing to plot their own advancement efforts into Central Asia. As originated under Russian Tsar Peter the Great, Russia continued his campaign for expansion and the establishment of Russian colonial territories in Asia. At the time, Britain was in control of India, and Russia was a constant threat on the horizon. Yet in spite of battling these other European powers, France also devised plans for the strategic purpose of establishing colonies in these regions. Napoleon Bonaparte of France was intrigued with Persia and so launched an attack on the British in India, even though his efforts to do the same from Egypt had failed. In 1800 and with the aid of Russia and Tsar Paul, Napoleon planned to invade India by way of Afghanistan.[8] However, the plan was ultimately thwarted by the assassination of Tsar Paul in 1801, and the British forces became aware of the potential Franco-Russian invasion that would have resulted in a disaster for the British. The enlightenment of this strategy was enough to alarm the

British to limit any further land threats into India, and this would ultimately intensify their stance with the politics and foreign affairs of Afghanistan. As a result, the prominent theme in the 19th-century in Afghanistan would be a call to holy war, or jihad, to protect the Islamic foundation in Afghanistan from these Christian infidels. As such, the Islamic call to a jihad would be launched against the Christian forces of the European powers of Russia and Britain. In these Islamic countries, it was deemed the sovereign duty of their respective leader to declare a jihad against the foreign invaders who tried to conquer their lands.[9] For the Pashtun tribes, the jihad was a call to support the *Pashtunwali*, the Pashtun Islamic religious code of honor and ethics.

Beginning his reign after his father's own unscrupulous rule, Zaman Shah faced many difficult challenges during his tenure as shah, which included the implementation of one monarch to rule all the Pashtun tribes amidst a severe lack of funding and tax revenue. In addition, he struggled with applying the Pashtuns' desire to rule without intervention and permission of the Pashtun tribal leaders. However, these ambitions were never achieved because of constant strife with the Sikhs. The Sikhs were continuously rebelling against the Pashtuns, and in an effort to finally gain control, Zaman Shah made the mistake of appointing a Sikh tribal chief to rule as governor of the Punjab region. Ranjit Singh was a dynamic and vigorous young Sikh chieftain, and the Afghan amir had hoped the appointment of Ranjit Singh would assist the Durrani Empire by ruling with the intention to subdue and to control the Sikhs. However, instead of reigning as a puppet monarch whose purpose was only to mollify the Sikhs from rebellion, this warrior chief used his position to become a fierce opponent to the Pashtun powers of Afghanistan.

Zaman Shah tried exhaustingly and overzealously to enforce his rule over the region, and ultimately his efforts to consolidate power led to his demise as the ruler of Afghanistan. Previously under Ahmad Shah's sovereignty, he had created a diplomatic equilibrium between the reigning leaders by placing all sects of the Durrani tribes into positions of power, as he did not want a council formed of despotic authority coming from one tribal clan. As such, this balanced system brought a sense of stability to Afghan supremacy and politics by ensuring that all tribal clans were equally represented. In his attempt to strengthen his control of the region—and especially the oppression of the Sikhs—Zaman Shah was determined to cease this harmonious council balance. He elected instead to remove the multiclan leaders and to institute new representatives from his own lineage of the Sadozai tribe. This action prompted the ousted Durrani leaders to conspire against Zaman Shah, led by Painda Khan Barakzai and other ejected Barakzai leaders. However, Zaman Shah thwarted the plan, and as a consequence of this insurgence, these newly instituted leaders were put to death. This execution included not only the chiefs of the Nurzai and Alizai Durrani clans but also the chief of the Qizilbash clan.

Zaman Shah's actions instilled conflict and confusion among the tribes, leading to an utter breakdown of governance and law. After the outbreak of chaos in 1801, Painda Khan's son Fatteh Khan (sometimes stated as Fateh or Fath Khan) fled to Iran to pledge alliance support to a new ruler of Afghanistan, Mahmud Shah. Mahmud was another of Timur's sons and also Zaman's older brother. After the execution of their leaders, these clans united with the rebelling forces and seized Kandahar from Zaman Shah. Mahmud Shah would begin his first reign for only two years until being ousted by Shuja Shah in 1803 when Shuja marched on the capital and seized Kabul. Recognizing he was outdone and defeated, Mahmud yielded the capital, and in addition he lost Kandahar because of his inability to control the Sunni revolts. Once more, Fatteh Khan fled the region and waited for the next opportunity to conduct an insurgence.

SHUJA SHAH DURRANI: 1803–1809

Shuja Shah Durrani ruled for six years amid the severe disorder and civil strife in Afghanistan and also during the continuous battle between the European powers. Most notably at the end of his reign, Shuja Shah signed a political and commercial treaty with the British in an effort to stop Persian aggression against the British and their territories. Britain desired to control the foreign policies of the country and constantly strove to maintain Afghanistan as a buffer state to halt aggression between France and Russia into India.[10] To secure these intentions, the British stipulated as part of the treaty that Shuja Shah must oppose any other foreign territories from passing though Afghanistan, indirectly implying that the most significant menaces were both France and Russia and their attempts at encroachment into India.

The treaty would be the first of many agreements with the European power, but soon after this contractual arrangement, his forerunner, Mahmud Shah, returned to overthrew Shuja Shah. The British would reinstate Shuja Shah again 30 years later during the First Anglo-Afghan Civil War, and he would reign again from 1839 to 1842 as a puppet monarch for the British. Until then and with the aid of Fatteh Khan once again, Mahmud seized Kandahar and Kabul in 1809. The ultimate defeat of Shuja Shah occurred at the Battle at Nimla located between Kabul and Peshawar, and Mahmud Shah was poised once more to be the ruler of Afghanistan.

MAHMUD SHAH: 1809–1818

As a reaction to the deplorable treaty Shuja had agreed to, Mahmud Shah Durrani reclaimed the throne of Afghanistan, reigning this time for nine years until 1818. Most notably, during his second reign he separated from the

The Durrani Empire through the Anglo-Afghan Wars

fgrough the Anglo-Afghan Wars**   **75**

Barakzai tribe after he apparently fell into disagreement with Fatteh Khan. The Afghan ruler ordered Fatteh to be blinded and executed by dismemberment, with no concern of Fatteh's assistance in championing Mahmud's return to the throne. However, despite the lapse in the original treaty between the British and the reinstated Afghan amir, British concern still lingered in relation to Afghanistan's foreign policy. The British wanted to secure their interests by confirming with the Afghan ruler that Afghanistan would remain a barrier country for any other European aggression. In 1814, the British returned to Afghanistan to request the shah to consent to another treaty. The terms were similar to the previous agreement under Shuja Shah but included an additional stipulation that would protect the British control of India. In this regard, the treaty specified that the Afghan ruler would not interact with or make any agreements with other countries that were the enemies of the British.[11]

Another son of Timur Shah, Sultan Ali Shah, briefly annexed the throne in 1818 and assumed the name Ali Shah Durrani. He ruled for only one year since the Sadozai rulers under Ahmad Shah Durrani were not able to control more than the city of Kabul. The Durrani line had lost control of all previously held territories, the result of which separated them from other tribes, and thus they were easily overthrown. However, because of Fatteh Khan's intelligent decision and influential control in Afghanistan, he had previously championed two of his brothers into prominent positions as the governors of Peshawar and Kandahar. Another of the younger Barakzai brothers, Dost Mohammad Khan, had worked his way into an influential position in Kabul. In the midst of the weakened empire, by 1826 Dost Mohammad was in prime position to take control of the Afghan kingdom.

EUROPEAN INFLUENCE IN AFGHANISTAN DURING 1826–1919—DOST MOHAMMAD KHAN: 1826–1839 AND 1843–1863

Dost Mohammed Khan was the younger brother of Fatteh Khan and was well aware that Fatteh had played a guiding role in helping Mahmud Khan achieve the seat of power in 1801 and again in 1809. Dost Mohammad would never forgive Mahmud for his brutal actions to have Fatteh blinded and killed in 1818, literally cutting him into pieces before Fatteh breathed his last. It was this revenge for his brother that fueled Dost Mohammad on his quest to power.[12] After his brother's atrocious death, Dost Mohammad advanced from Kashmir and annexed the fortress of Peshawar and Kabul. After a bloody conflict, Mahmud was forced to abandon all control over his regions except for Herat, and the remaining provinces were divided among Fatteh's brothers. Dost Mohammed Khan was allocated control of Ghazni and now controlled Kabul and Jalalabad as well. In 1826, he assumed the title of amir in Kabul and founded the Barakzai (Barakzay) dynasty in Afghanistan, thus bringing an end to the Durrani line. As soon as Dost Mohammad began his rule, he was engaged in conflict with Ranjit Singh, the Sikh ruler of the Punjab as established by Zaman Shah. After several years, in 1834 and under the oversight of Ranjit Singh, the once-dethroned Shuja Shah attempted to reclaim his kingdom. In 1836, Dost Mohammad declared a jihad and defeated Shuja Shah at Kandahar, but the distraction allowed Ranjit Singh to successfully capture and assume control of the fortress of Peshawar, a feat that would prove troublesome for the Afghan amir.

THE FIRST ANGLO-AFGHAN WAR: 1838–1842

The competition for territory in Central Asia began in the early 18th century with the British and the Russians each racing for mastery in these lands. However, in the early 19th century, events would catapult the clash into the British invasion of Afghanistan. As implemented under the reign of Zaman Shah, the main objective of the British imperialists was to control Afghanistan by keeping the country weak and therefore dependent on the British government.[13] As was the situation in 1836, Dost Mohammad had removed Shuja Shah from power, thus removing the British figurehead and puppet monarch as established by the treaty in 1809. The British tired to secure a new friendship with Dost Mohammad in an effort to retain the Afghan's amicable favoritism to the British occupation of Afghanistan. However, Dost Mohammad was resolute in his stance of Afghan independence from foreign occupation and refused to allow the British to roam at will throughout his state. He no longer agreed with the British treaty as signed by Shuja Shah to not allow other countries (namely, Russia) to pass through Afghanistan. Gradually, the British began to hear of Dost Mohammad's interaction with the Russians, and the Persians, as part of the ruler's endeavor to signify the British treaty, would no longer be part of Afghan policy.

However, in 1837 Dost Mohammad attempted to form an alliance with Britain in the hopes of capturing Peshawar, and in turn the British Captain Alexander Burnes was invited to Kabul. The British were willing to discuss and outline the strategic alliance against Ranjit Singh, but before doing so Dost Mohammad would have to retract any agreements with other European powers. At the time, Mohammad Shah of Persia was trying to capture Herat, which the British knew was the strategic foothold to gain entrance to India. Burnes arrived as a representative of Lord Auckland, the British governor-general of India, and also to represent the British interventionist diplomat Sir William Macnaghten. As such, the British swore to protect Dost Mohammad from Ranjit Singh if he ceased his attempts to recover Peshawar. Burnes would not offer the assurances Dost Mohammad needed, and instead Burnes insisted that the Afghan amir should place Afghan policy and control under British guidance. Recognizing the conundrum of his situation, Dost Mohammad rejected the British and quickly sought to form an alliance with Russia. On the cusp of Burnes's failure to subdue Afghanistan, the situation was further intensified on witnessing the Russian emissary Lieutenant Vitkievitch in Kabul. The British retreated to India, and in 1838 Lord Auckland declared war on Afghanistan.[14]

The First Anglo-Afghan War had officially begun, and in February 1839 the British forces advanced through the Bolan Pass of the Toba Kakar range in Pakistan, approximately 120 miles from the Afghani border. By late April, the army arrived in Kandahar to find that the Afghan princes had abandoned the area. Lord Auckland achieved his preliminary goal and restored the now quite elderly Shuja Shah to the throne as amir of Afghanistan. Dost Mohammad had previously fled the capital city and was forced to retreat into the Hindu Kush Mountains. Among the harsh terrain and extreme weather, Dost Mohammad and his supporters sought evasion in the caves of the mountains for nearly a year as the British intently pursued him. Finally weary of the advancing forces, Dost Mohammad surrendered to the British on the evening of November 4, 1840, by allegedly riding on horseback up to General Macnaghten and offering his amicable surrender. As prisoner, he was held in captivity during the British occupation of Afghanistan, and Dost Mohammed would be released after the recapture of Kabul in the fall of 1842.

By the end of 1841 and after having to endure watching their ruler be ousted and imprisoned by the British forces, the Afghan tribes rallied to support Dost Mohammad's son Mohammad Akbar Khan. Over the following months, the British forces faced numerous revolts and bloody executions, including the murder of Sir Alexander Burnes and his aides by an angry horde in Kabul. After the attack, General Macnaghten tried to negotiate with Mohammad Akbar Khan to allow the British to remain in the country, but in a severe act of defiance against the British, Mohammad Akbar ordered Macnaghten thrown in prison. Macnaghten never made it to his confinement, for on his march to the prison he was attacked and dismembered by a livid Afghan crowd. As a gesture of their intolerance of any more British occupation in their country, the mob triumphantly paraded his dead and nearly limbless corpse around the streets of Kabul. The British recognized the severity of their situation in Afghanistan, and in January 1842 they reached an agreement to provide the immediate retreat of the British forces out of Afghanistan. As the exodus began, the British troops struggled through the snowbound passes and were ambushed by Ghilzai tribesmen. Along the treacherous pass between Kabul and Gandamak, almost 16,000 British soldiers and supporters were attacked and ruthlessly slaughtered. Only one survivor arrived at the British outpost in Jalalabad to describe the tale, and by that point Dr. William Brydon was barely breathing and slumped over his horse with only a faint trace of life left in his body.[15] The horrifying massacre was enough to rejuvenate the British to return later in the year to relieve the British garrison at Jalalabad and rescue any remaining British occupants and prisoners in the country. The loss of life and property in Afghanistan, including the destruction of the *bazaar* (marketplace) in Kabul, resulted in a severe hatred of foreign occupation that is ingrained in the culture of Afghanistan to this day.

Often referred to by the British as "Auckland's Folly" because of Lord Auckland's erroneous judgments and decisions against the Afghan people, the First Anglo-Afghan Civil War from 1839 to 1842 resulted in the destruction of the British army, including the loss of nearly 20,000 soldiers and 50,000 camels and costs upward of £20 million.[16] Further, the defeat and refusal of British hegemony attests to the Afghans' fierce resistance to foreign invaders attempting to occupy their lands. By the end of the first British invasion and Afghan war, Shah Shuja was presumably assassinated in 1842. After several months of chaos in Kabul, Mohammad Khan was able to secure control of the city until his father Dost Mohammad was set free at the decision of the British government to abandon the control of internal politics in Afghanistan. On his return from Hindustan, Dost Mohammad was welcomed back to the seat of power in Kabul, and in April 1843 Dost Mohammad resumed his title as king. Over the next decade, Dost Mohammad would work at resuming control of the regions of Mazar-e-Sharif, Konduz, Badakshan, and Kandahar.

On his return to power, Dost Mohammad set forth with plans to implement his authority and control against the British. In support of his regime, he once again sought to defeat the Sikhs, who were engaged in combat with the British. In 1848, Dost Mohammad seized the opportunity to take control of Peshawar. However, in February 1849 his army was defeated at Gujarat, and he abandoned his previous intentions to control Peshawar. After he led troops back into Afghanistan, Dost Mohammad realized that he would not be successful in his actions to capture Peshawar, and he abandoned any further efforts to do so. By concentrating on other regions, Dost Mohammad conquered Balkh a year later and furthermore, in 1854, captured Kandahar and successfully assumed control over the southern Afghan tribes.

In retaliation for the humiliation endured in the First Anglo-Afghan War, the British attacked Afghanistan again, but this time the onslaught included a large Indian force. After several battles, new British forces relieved the previous Jalalabad garrison and then advanced into Kabul, destroying the central bazaar and the large citadel. By 1854, the British were ready to recommence associations with Afghanistan. In the following year, the British opened up diplomatic relations with Afghanistan in the Treaty of Peshawar. The treaty recognized the authority of each country and additionally acknowledged each county's territorial boundaries. In doing so, the treaty declared henceforth a British–Afghan relationship of amenity in political interaction and unity in defeating enemies. On March 30, 1855, the Afghan leader agreed to the alliance with the British government, and as a specification of the treaty the province of Herat was placed in control of the Barakzai sovereignty. The coalition of the Afghans with the British resulted in both forces declaring war on Persia in 1857. During the period of Indian Mutiny in Afghanistan, Dost Mohammad abstained from supporting the uprising rebels despite the call for jihad in which the Sikhs were supporters of India's movement against British occupation. Two years later in 1857, the treaty was amended so that while the British were fighting with the Iranians, Afghanistan's parliament would allow the British military to maintain a presence at Kandahar. The Iranians had previously attacked Herat in 1856, and as such Dost Mohammad was eager to accept the terms in the addendum.

While America was fighting its own civil war, Dost Mohammad's final years were troubled with revolts out of Herat and Bokhara. In 1863, he personally led the Afghan army with the British troops at his flank, driving the Persian army from Kandahar. As a result of the treaty's allowance for the British presence, Dost Mohammad was able to seize back Herat from the Iranians only a few months before his death. On May 26, 1863, Dost Mohammad and his Afghan army captured Herat for good, but surprisingly Dost Mohammad died suddenly in the midst of his triumph. During his life, he played a pivotal role in shaping Central Asia and Afghanistan, and on his death his son Sher Ali Khan had been appointed heir to the kingdom.

SHER ALI: 1863–1866 AND 1868–1879

At the time of Sher Ali's enthronement, his older brother, Mohammad Afzal, was in power at Kabul. By the time Sher Ali had taken control of Kabul, the British government once again viewed Afghanistan as a buffer state. As such, the British were willing to support Sher Ali's regime financially and with weapons rather than sending troops to provide the much-needed physical support forces. Sher Ali was not able to succeed in his father's quest and recapture Kabul until 1868. While once joined as a united team, over the next 10 years the relationship between the two governments deteriorated rapidly. Increasingly over the years, the Afghan ruler was leery of the Russians advancement into Afghanistan. In May 1873, led by Russian General Von Kaufman, the Russians attacked the city of Khiva. By the early 17th century, Khiva had been established as the prominent capital of the Khanate of Khiva, located in modern Uzbekistan. The Russians were now in control of the khanate, and frighteningly close to attempting the same in Afghanistan. While the Russians were trying to advance into Afghanistan, the Afghan ruler called on his British counterparts to provide support.

THE SECOND ANGLO-AFGHAN WAR: 1878–1880

Unbeknownst to Sher Ali, the British has signed an agreement with the Russians the previous year stating that the Russians agreed to respect the boundaries of Afghanistan. Upholding the terms of the previously signed treaty, the British did not provide any support to Afghanistan and furthermore would not provide any promises or reassurance to Sher Ali. After the Congress of Berlin in June 1878, Russia sent an uninvited representative to Kabul whom Sher Ali tried to refuse. The Russians tried to persuade the shah to accept their visit by offering such enticements as offering troop support against the British and offering to build roads and install telegraph lines. No longer able to defer the encounter and with reluctance, Sher Ali finally succumbed and turned to his Russian associates. However, once the British verified the existence of a Russian envoy in Kabul, the British demanded that the Afghan ruler welcome a British diplomat as well. The British persistence was meant to counter the Russians' insistence on visiting Kabul, which, through intelligence and the interception of mail correspondence, the British had known the Russians had been attempting for a number of years. Again, Sher Ali refused, but the British insisted that they too needed to visit the Afghani amir and even proceeded with sending the British envoy forward into Kabul. The troops were intercepted at the Khyber Pass and instructed not to proceed further, or they would be met with a resilient Afghan force. Once the British were refused at the eastern entrance of the Khyber Pass and forced to turn back, this was the unofficial commencement of the Second Anglo-Afghan War.

The rebuke resulted in the British cabinet declaring war on Afghanistan. Sher Ali was given the opportunity to grant a British summit once again, and while allowing the Afghan leader three weeks to make a decision, General Britton moved ahead with his military planning. Lasting for two years, the Second Anglo-Afghan Civil War began when the British marched into Afghanistan in August 1878. The British plan for invasion and political usurpation was to divide the army into three forces and invading Afghanistan at three different locations. Unable to gain support, Sher Ali retreated to Mazar-e-Sharif and died on February 21, 1879.

YAQUB KHAN: 1879

The British had invaded much of the country when Sher Ali's son Yaqub Khan succeeded him. In return for Jalalabad and Kandahar and with little option, Yaqub signed the Treaty of Gandamak in May 1879 to prevent the British from conquering the remaining provinces of Afghanistan. Perhaps in fear of the first Afghan War, Yaqub agreed to outlandish stipulations that in essence gave the British control over Afghanistan, and furthermore Yaqub ceded the lands of Pishin and Sibi. The treaty also included multiple stipulations, such as that British authority would be physically represented in Kabul and other cities, British control would include the Khyber Pass and also the Michni Pass, and Afghanistan must release certain frontier lands to the British. Once the Afghan people realized the magnitude of the agreement, which included releasing all control in the foreign affairs of Afghanistan to the British, the strong-willed Afghan population rebelled against their ruler.

In September 1879, the Afghan insurgence killed the British emissary and his escort while they were stationed in Kabul, and in fear Yaqub fled the throne under the guise of British amnesty. British forces marched into central Afghanistan and simultaneously defeated the Afghan army in October and then restored Yaqub to the throne. By March of the following year, the British realized that controlling Afghanistan as a buffer state would require controlling the dissenting Afghan people, and even defeating them did not mean they had overpowered their strong-willed spirits. Knowing full well of the continuous threat of rebellions and uprising and recognizing the disastrous experiences of their British predecessors in the First Anglo-Afghan War, the British finally realized they could not control Afghanistan.[17] The British implemented the removal of Yaqub Khan and the induction of Amir Abdur Rahman to the throne of Afghanistan, with Britain retaining control of Kabul's foreign policies and interactions.

ABDUR RAHMAN KHAN, "THE IRON AMIR": 1880–1901

In 1881, the British removed their forces from Afghanistan, but not before offering Abdur Rahman Khan the throne and requiring the new amir to uphold the Treaty of Gandamak. Despite gaining a minor amount of territory and influence in Afghanistan, the British knew that the Afghan people would embrace Abdur Rahman Khan since he was the nephew of Sher Ali, and he would also remain loyal to the influence of the British and conduct Afghanistan's foreign policy through the government of India. During Amir Abdur's 20-year reign from 1880 to 1901, the British and the Russians established the official boundaries and territorial lines of present-day Afghanistan.

Additionally during his reign, the British established several corps of the Northwest Frontier Province, which were set up to protect this region from invasion. Previously under the British invasion of Afghanistan, the Khyber Rifles was one of eight "frontier corps" that served as auxiliaries for the British Indian army and was one of the oldest military units of the Northwest Frontier Province. The corps began as an assembly of Afridi tribesmen known as the Khyber Jezailchis in November 1878 led by Captain Gais Ford, and he commanded until 1881, when the regiment was turned over to Mohammad Aslam Khan. The British commanders from Indian regiments were the primary leaders, and the Afridis were established as the second line of command. Under Mohammad Aslam's 16-year reign as commander from 1881 to 1897, the corps changed from the Khyber Jezailchis to the Khyber Rifles and would henceforth support all areas rather than the previous support to only the Khyber Agency. The Khyber Rifles established their command center of operations at Landi Kotal, and the main purpose of the regiment was simply to guard the Khyber Pass. The brigade included three main strongholds of the Khyber Pass, which included the primary location at Landi Kotal on the western end. The other two major command centers included Fort Maude on the eastern side and Ali Masjid in the center of the Khyber Pass.[18] Unification of the corps was vital, and to symbolize their objective, the badge was emblazoned with two crossed Afghan daggers encircled with the name "Khyber Rifles."

The Durand Line issue began in 1893 and would take more than four years to negotiate because of the constant difficulties in the delineation and the feelings of resentment the Durand Line created. From the Afghan point of view, the implementation of the Durand Line would mean Afghanistan would remain a landlocked nation and would never have access to a seaport. Abdur Rahman had little choice after four years in the signing of the treaty, and in spite of his hand being forced by the British, the citizens of Afghanistan would never forgive the Iron Amir for signing such an agreement. However, he is widely renowned as a popular figure for creating a unified kingdom that was circumscribed of tribal authority. His reputation was hindered by his resolution of the Durand Line issue, his encouragement of brutal torture and execution methods to force rebellions tribes to submit to the law, and his lack of implementing social and economic reforms.

Throughout his reign, Abdur Rahman's goal was to break down these tribal alliances and institute one nation under one rule, and during his reign, he endured and crushed more than 40 tribal revolts. By furthering his regime and earning him the title of "The Iron Amir," he enforced the migration of 10,000 Ghilzai families to relocate in an effort to break apart the tribal structure that had formed in the Hindu Kush Mountains. Furthermore, he restricted the movement of migrating tribes so that the tribes could not relocate without the approval of the Afghan government, and in doing so he further suppressed the Hazara tribes from revolt. While toiling to implement his command for ethnic cleansing and relocation of ethnic tribes, there was little money left in the vaults of the treasury, and he ordered tax collectors to collect the revenue across Afghanistan. These tax payments were difficult for the disenchanted relocated tribes, and those who revolted against the payment of taxes were brutally punished. By the time of his death in 1901, Abdur Rahman had successfully subdued tribal revolts so that he could control the country, and he additionally developed a spy and informant network to assist his monitoring of tribal actions and any planned insurgency, including the use of Afghanistan's first secret police force.[19] Interestingly enough, he was against such technological advancements as the telephone and the railroad, as he believed these advancements would be a way for the British to move troops into Afghanistan.

HABIBOLLAH KHAN: 1901–1919

In a unique turn of events in Afghanistan, Habibollah Khan's ascension to the throne was peaceful and was not contested after Abdur Khan's death. On commencement of his reign, Habibollah's regime would prove to be much different than his fathers, and as such his tenure in office is regarded one of severe neutrality. In stark contrast to his father, Habibollah abolished his father's spy system on Afghan tribes and foreign countries. Furthermore, Habibollah Khan is regarded as a progressive thinker who sought to establish a modern land with advancements in technology, education, and medicine. Despite his dominating policy of noninvolvement in World War I, he is credited with opening the technology portal for Afghanistan by introducing such innovations as electricity and the automobile.

Overall, the country of Afghanistan remained neutral during World War I despite the encouragement of the Germans to persuade the Afghans into anti-British sentiment and action. Regardless of the Germans efforts to create a British rebellion in Afghanistan, most notably along the borders of British India, it was the sovereign choice of the King of Afghanistan to remain nonaligned in the war even with the main sentiment toward British rule. Habibollah Khan treated the affairs of World War I with indifference and announced early on that Afghanistan would remain neutral. Rather than focusing on outside affairs, Habibollah desired to focus on the internal aspects of the country and sought to modernize and advance Afghanistan. For this reason, Habibollah Khan worked to pacify tribal schisms in Afghanistan, and in support of this regime he instituted a tribal state council to monitor tribal affairs. Despite the efforts of Lord Curzon in India to engage the Afghan leader in the war, Habibollah Khan was able to stall the British from a meeting for three years by arguing he could not abandon the throne of Kabul for such a rendezvous. As a result of his lack of engagement, Lord Curzon sought permission of the London cabinet to declare war and authorize an invasion of Afghanistan. After the British cabinet overruled this effort, Habibollah continued the neutral stance, much to the chagrin of his British counterparts and Afghan council. However, his neutrality would change once Turkey became confrontational toward Afghanistan. In September 1915, a Turko-German mission arrived in Kabul that left Habibollah Khan anxious and unsettled.[20] Yet in spite of these foreign pressures and the implicit internal call to jihad, Habibollah Khan continued to insist that Afghanistan would remain neutral.

As a result of his penchant for impartiality and a nonaligned status, the country endured a widespread belief that by his actions to remain neutral he was not supporting Afghanistan's ideology of Islamic beliefs. Habibollah Khan failed to conciliate not only the war party but also the religious, political, and tribal leaders. Habibollah Khan was assassinated in 1919, presumably by family members who were resistant to British influence and control. Not much was achieved during his reign, as he was affected by severely limited financial capital, but he at least was able to begin the movement of social and economic reforms that would be further implemented and blossom under the hands of his successor, Amanullah Khan.

NOTES

1. Peter Hopkirk, *The Great Game: The Struggle for Empire in Central Asia.* The British intelligence officer Arthur Conolly is originally credited with coining the term "The Great Game" in a letter he wrote to Sir Henry Rawilnson in 1829. Conolly served in many British reconnaissance missions in Central Asia, and he often traveled in disguise and used the name Khan Ali, a play on his last name. British novelist and poet Rudyard Kipling glamorized the term in his work *Kim* written in 1901, in which the novel is set during the competitive movement in the 19th century for territory between two of the world's supreme powers, Great Britain and Russia. Originally referred to as the "Afghan Wars," the title was changed to "Anglo-Afghan Wars" in the late 20th century to differentiate these earlier wars from the multiple successive Afghan civil wars that have occurred since the Soviet invasion of 1979.

2. Senzil K. Nawid, *Religious Response to Social Change in Afghanistan 1919–29.* The beginning of the Durrani Empire is regarded as the beginning of modern Afghanistan.

3. Stephen Tanner, *Afghanistan: A Military History from Alexander the Great to the Fall of the Taliban.* In spite of the speculations about why the young Ahmad Shah was appointed the primary candidate for the throne, a holy man named Mohammad Sabir Khan championed him for the throne. The holy leader argued that Ahmad was already a proven commander and that his tribal affiliation would be beneficial in reducing clan opposition.

4. Nawid, *Religious Response to Social Change in Afghanistan 1919–29.* Ahmad Shah's victories in these prominent battles would thrust him to the center of Afghan power as a military commander, an Islamic leader, and also by his courageous call for jihad.

5. Martin Ewans, *Afghanistan: A Short History of Its People and Politics.* It is believed that Ahmad Shah Durrani's health had been failing because of skin

cancer. On his death in 1772, he was placed in a mausoleum in Kandahar, one of the highly respected sites in Afghanistan.

6. Hafizullah Emadi, *Culture and Customs of Afghanistan.* Timur had between 23 and 26 sons, with some accounts simply stating "over 20 sons," as it has been historically difficult to determine the exact count. Tanner, in *Afghanistan,* references that Timur had at least 30 sons and possibly more who are not accounted for in Timur's harem, but regardless of the exact count, the number was so great that, with no named heir to the throne, he left the kingdom in chaos.

7. Ewans, *Afghanistan,* It is said that Zaman Shah had imprisoned all but two of his brothers and forced them into compliance by starvation. Humayan was the oldest of Timur's sons and also the governor of Kandahar, and as such he was the greatest competitor. For these reasons, Zaman ordered Humayan to be blinded for conspiring to assume the throne, and the incident would eliminate him as a threat to the new amir.

8. Bernard Lewis, *The Middle East: A Brief History of the Last 2,000 Years.* The author discusses in further detail France's intentions for controlling the region.

9. Nawid, *Religious Response to Social Change in Afghanistan 1919–29.* The jihad call to arms to defend Islamic rule unified the multitude of tribes and ethnicities. For many, the true potency and valor of a leader is in his willingness to declare a jihad for defense of the country.

10. Lewis, *The Middle East.* The British were constantly seeking to administer and control the political and foreign affairs of Afghanistan.

11. Lewis, *The Middle East.* Persia would be granted a yearly subsidy for upholding the treaty and not engaging in any other wars or aggressions. The subsidy agreement was terminated in 1827 after aggressions escalated between Persia and Russia.

12. Ewans, *Afghanistan.* Both Dost Mohammad and Fatteh Khan marched into Herat in 1817, and Dost Mohammad had been instructed to seize the city. Interestingly enough, somehow Dost Mohammad found his way into the Saddozi harem, where he allegedly tore off the jeweled *perjamas* belt of the prince's wife. For this insult, Dost Mohammad's actions were part of the reason for Fatteh Khan's brutal death and thus served as inspiration for Dost Mohammad to defeat the Afghan ruler.

13. Abdul Ghaffar Farahi, *Afghanistan during Democracy and Republic: 1963–1978.* The goal of the British was to weaken Afghanistan and thus block any further development in the country, which would make it easier for the British to control the country.

14. For additional details on the intricacies behind the Dost Mohammad's plans with the Russians and the Persians, see Karl E. Meyer, *The Dust of Empire: The Race for Mastery in the Asian Heartland,* and Ewans, *Afghanistan,* in

which the author states that Dost Mohammad was only trying to pressure the British to abandon any controlling intentions with Afghanistan by inviting the Russian lieutenant to Kabul.

15. Tanner, *Afghanistan*. The author describes a fascinating account and description of the massacre of the British soldiers and the escape of Dr. Brydon facing the Afghan warriors.

16. Ewans, *Afghanistan*. In addition to these tangible costs of war instigated by Lord Auckland, as a further embarrassment the British lost substantial respect in India of the war's outcome.

17. Ewans, *Afghanistan*. Even working to finance the war, Yaqub Khan's mother handed over her jewel to finance food for the troops.

18. Jules Stewart, *The Khyber Rifles: From the British Raj to Al Qaeda*.

19. Ewans, *Afghanistan*. This secret police under Rahman was a forerunner to KHAD during the Soviet occupation of the 1980s.

20. Ewans, *Afghanistan*. As justification for his neutral stance, he did not want to risk any further aggression with Russia and Britain.

7

From the Age of Reformation
to the War with the Soviets,
1919–1979

As the sentiment of Afghan nationalism began to rise, the assassination of Habibollah Khan in February 1919 may be regarded as the first monumental political step toward the formation of a constitutional government in Afghanistan. Previously under King Habibollah's government, a social group of intellectuals known as "The Young Afghans" supported the contrasting viewpoint of the anti-British occupation movement and the modernization of the country. Throughout Habibollah's reign, the Afghan amir's stance of pro-British occupation primarily contributed to the increased sentiment of aggravation with the Afghan government. This frustration gave birth to the modernization movement in the early 20th century initiated by Mahmud Tarzi, an influential writer and champion of Afghan freedom, which he promoted through his articles and publications. To an extent, King Habibollah practiced some form of modernism and was tolerant of these political articles as long as these freedom-laced writings did not produce an insurgence. After ruling with this policy of tolerance for a number of years, Habibollah became outraged in 1916 at Tarzi's call to the nation to rise up and defeat the British in defense of Islam. Tarzi's criticism of European dominance in the nation, coupled with Afghanistan's stance of neutrality in World War I, was well received by the young Prince Amanullah, and his support of the influential writer even resulted in marriage to Tarzi's daughter in 1916.[1]

SOCIAL REFORMATION IN AFGHANISTAN UNDER AMANULLAH KHAN: 1919–1929

The assassination of King Habibollah occurred while he was on a hunting trip in February 1919, presumably killed by his family members because of his refusal to support Turkey against Britain. Shortly after the assassination, the king's brother Nasrullah promptly assumed the kingship, and both of young Amanullah's older brothers supported this arrangement. However, in Kabul, Prince Amanullah emerged as the new champion and defender of Islamic freedom and independence. While his uncle had already assumed the kingship, within several days Amanullah was thrust to the forefront by declaring that Nasrullah was involved in the assassination of the king. Further, Amanullah declared that his brothers had abandoned their rights to the throne by supporting their uncle and his heinous acts, and consequently, Amanullah vowed to seek vengeance for his usurped father. As a result, two political parties championed for the throne, one led by Amanullah and the other by Nasrullah. While both groups were united in the fight against British occupation, the king's brother supported the orthodox political movement, whereas Amanullah supported Afghan nationalism. The result cast Amanullah in the prime position for the throne since by discrediting his uncle he gained the support of Afghan nationalists and the Afghan nobility who were allied with King Habibollah.

THIRD ANGLO-AFGHAN WAR AND AUTONOMY

King Amanullah was resolute in his stance on Afghan autonomy from foreign control. Over the past 40 years in Afghanistan, since the Second Anglo-Afghan War, the boundaries of the country had been devised by foreign governments and their desire to implement Afghanistan as a buffer state. The various treaties and agreements over the years, some of which Afghanistan was forced to comply with, instilled Amanullah's implementation of a regime to create a nation composed of independent rule. The British-imposed Treaty of Gandamak in 1879 and the application of the Durand Line in 1893 forced British control and influence in Afghanistan. On the opposite side of the Great Game, the Russians imposed the settlement of the lands of the Amu-Darya in 1888 and also the 1895 settlement of Parmir. These frontiers had been established for Afghanistan by foreign governments with no respect for the tribal ethnic boundaries and the Muslim faith, and as a result this foreign directed allocation of boundaries was deeply resented.[2]

Amanullah launched the Third Anglo-Afghan War in May 1919 by attacking India with the intention to finally gain control over Afghanistan's foreign policy. Previously, during the Russian Revolution in 1917, Afghanistan served again as the battleground for the Russians and the British who were simultaneously vying for control in the Asian heartland. After growing tired of this repetitive pattern, King Amanullah desired to implement reforms in Afghanistan that could be accomplished only by finally attaining Afghan independence from the British. In this regard, King Amanullah sought to finalize Afghanistan's independence in May 1919 by surprising the British in an attack, and the British retaliated with an aerial assault in which King Amanullah's house was attacked. The incident is the first aerial invasion in Afghanistan's history and forced a truce known as the Treaty of Rawalpindi, the details of which were so complicated that the final details of the treaty took nearly two years to complete through negotiations.[3] In the treaty, the British recognized Afghan independence and agreed that the British kingdom would not extend beyond the Khyber Pass. Before completion of the treaty in 1921, the Afghan ruler had already established foreign relations with most major countries, including Russia, which was outside of British coordination. Without question, the Khyber Pass was of the utmost strategic importance during these negotiations and agreements. Despite how long it took to resolve the document, the Treaty of Rawalpindi symbolizes Afghan independence and the end of the Great Game between the Russian and the British empires, and August 19, 1919, is commemorated as Afghanistan's Independence Day. After nearly 60 years of fighting against British oppression, Afghanistan successfully fought for and won its freedom from British control and influence. By signing the Treaty of Rawalpindi, the war-weary British relinquished control of Afghanistan, not just territorially but also in any other affairs, both internal and foreign. This noteworthy agreement opened the door for King Amanullah to finally begin the age of reformation in Afghanistan. After 10 years as the Afghan ruler, his social, economic, and political reforms infiltrated not only Afghanistan's domestic dealings but foreign relations as well.

While both parties agreed on Afghan independence as stipulated in the first treaty, the debate and peace negotiations continued into a second deliberation since both parties could not agree on the territorial boundaries of the Durand Line. This cartographical delineation represented a division of the British and Afghan control of the Pashtun tribes and ultimately was designed to act as a British buffer zone against further Russian aggression and encroachment into India. Delineated in 1893 and reluctantly agreed to by Amir Abdur Rahman in 1897, the meandering Durand Line had detached the eastern Pashtun tribes near Pakistan from Afghanistan and created what would be referred to as the Pashtunian issue. The Durand Line was implemented based on a cartographic representation of Afghanistan and Pakistan, and the line was arbitrarily drawn without any consideration for existing physical structures, property rights, or ethnicity and family locations.[4] The ethnographic Durand

Line had been a cause for friction among the Anglo-Afghan empires for many years, and the continual debate in 1921 still would not resolve the issue, as the British refused to abandon their control and simultaneously the Afghans were unrelenting on the agreement. Hence, in Afghanistan, the compromise in 1921 was regarded as a merely informal agreement on a continually unsettled issue. In addition, during this Third Anglo-Afghan War, the loyalty of the Khyber Rifles was put under severe strain, leading to the desertion of many members, including nearly 1,200 sepoys.[5] In consequence, the Khyber Rifles was disbanded for being unreliable and capricious and would not be reinstated until World War II.

While the British and the Afghans were struggling to finalize their independence agreement, the Russians moved forward with establishing amicable relations with Afghanistan. The Bolshevik Revolution of 1917 led to dramatic changes in the Russian government and also in the pacification efforts of their Muslim inhabitants. As such, the Soviet government sought to establish amicable relationships with neighboring Islamic countries to mollify any uprisings from the Muslim population in Russia. In this regard, the Russians were eager to befriend the Afghan leader in Kabul not only for the pacification of the Muslim minority in Russia but also to create an Afghan–Soviet allegiance that would serve as a threat to Britain. Upholding his beliefs in Afghan independence from the British, Amanullah sent an emissary to meet with Vladimir Lenin in Moscow. The Afghan representative was warmly welcomed, and in response Lenin sent his own representative to provide support and aid to Afghanistan. The relationship between the two empires fluctuated between the Soviets' use of Afghanistan as a pawn in their anti-Bolshevik relationships in Central Asia and as an allegiance threat to the British. Meanwhile, the Afghans merely wanted Soviets to abandon control over territory across the Amu Darya that was previously lost to the Russians in the early 19th century. In the first act of establishing foreign relations since winning their independence in August 1919, the Soviets and the Afghans signed a cordial Treaty of Friendship in May 1921. Despite the Soviets' efforts and provisions for such gifts as technological advancements and military equipment such as King Amanullah's highly desired Soviet aircraft, Amanullah was displeased with the growing oppression of the Islamic minority in Russia. Nevertheless, Anglo-Afghan relations gradually dwindled because of the newly founded Afghan-Soviet friendship. While his efforts with the Soviets had increased, Amanullah's amicable relationship with the British was rapidly descending into a large maelstrom. Recognizing this disparity, the British responded by increasing the restrictions on the shipment of goods through India.

While the atmosphere of Afghanistan's affairs with Britain were unsteady and with Russian concordance in the early stages, Amanullah continued his goal of instituting several reforms in Afghanistan, including social, economic, and political reforms. In a new era after the dawn of Afghan independence, King Amanullah sought to eliminate Afghanistan's traditional role of isolation and seclusion from neighboring countries. Following the Third Anglo-Afghan War, Amanullah recognized the need to establish diplomatic relations with several major countries. After an influential tour of Europe and Turkey in 1927 in which he witnessed firsthand how these governments operated, he instituted several reforms in an effort to modernize Afghanistan under a strong central government.[6] King Amanullah's foreign minister and father-in-law, Mahmud Tarzi, was a driving force and pivotal component for instituting and developing these reforms. Furthermore, Mahmud Tarzi was an avid supporter of the education and advancement of women. In this regard, he intently fought for and won a constitutional legislative law that made elementary education in Afghanistan mandatory. His daughter, Queen Soraya Tarzi, was a driving force and the political face of championing women independence in Afghanistan. Queen Soraya was a prominent ruler for her pioneering efforts in the women's rights movement in Afghanistan. She was a devout supporter of the enlightenment period for women, and her efforts have often given her the distinction of being the first and one of the most powerful Afghani female activists. Her feminine-based advancement efforts included such reforms as education for females and the inclusion of women in political activities.

The king continued implementing his revolutionary judicial and political reformation efforts. Most notably, in 1923 he instituted the First Constitution of Afghanistan and furthermore implemented a code of civil rights for the Afghan people. Amanullah also instituted a system of national identification through registration and citizen identification cards. In the judicial improvements, he established a legislative assembly and a court system with multiple factions of code enforcement, and he even further eradicated subsidized payments that were granted to tribal chiefs. However, these revolutionary concepts were not met with excitement, and as such many orders established under Habibollah Khan were alienated by some of Amanullah's efforts, including religious leaders.

As a respected leader, King Amanullah is regarded as a modern thinker who successfully initiated many reforms, but most of his ideas never achieved full fruition. He transformed Afghanistan by bringing the country into the 20th century with his social, economic, and political reforms. In this manner, he was successful in achieving such social reforms as adopting the Western style of dress, the elimination of the veiled headdress for women, and the abolishment of slavery and forced labor. His education reforms included secular education for both young men and young women, and he further instituted education policies for nomads and farmers. Over the tenure of his reign, influenced largely by his Uncle Sardar Mohammad Hashim Khan, who previously served as the prime minister under Nadir Shah. During his last decade of rule, Zadir's reign would be independent from the sovereign advisement and oversight of his family.

Soon after establishing his sovereignty as king, his Uncle Hashim guided King Zahir to make decisions for the nation. Afghanistan became acknowledged in the world by joining the League of Nations in 1934, and subsequently Afghanistan was also officially recognized as a country by the United States. Afghanistan established a new government with the objective of strengthening the army, the economy, the transportation system, and the methods of communication in Afghanistan. However, in order to successfully implement and achieve these goals, Hashim knew this would require the aid of foreign countries. After the long history of the Great Game, Hashim was reluctant to turn to Britain and the Soviet Union. Instead, the Afghan government sought new relations with Germany, and by 1935 a multitude of German factories and business projects existed in Afghanistan. Other projects and development efforts were initiated with Japan and Italy. The Treaty of Saadabad on July 9, 1937, established additional relations with neighboring countries. The treaty was a nonaggression pact that increased Afghanistan's regional ties with the Islamic states of Iran, Iraq, and Turkey and lasted for five years.

In the early stages of World War II, Afghanistan quickly announced its neutrality in the war on August 17, 1940. However, in spite of this declaration of impartiality, the Allied forces were displeased with the allowance and tolerance of German personnel stationed in Afghanistan. In this regard, the Allied forces of the British and Russians insisted that Afghanistan expel from its borders any nondiplomatic people who were representatives of the Axis countries. Despite his feelings of insult at this request, King Zahir requested loya jirga, where he once again reiterated the Afghan stance on neutrality in the war, but he eventually ordered the Afghan government to comply with the Allied request.

Shortly after the end of World War I, in 1946, another of Zahir Shah's uncles replaced the prime minister. After taking the place of his older brother, Sardar Shah Mahmud Khan tried to implement both internal and external policies with the intention of initiating a period of great change in Afghanistan. One such policy regarded political freedom, but he was forced to abort the strategy once it had spun out of his control, and as a consequence he was forced to overturn any beneficial results from the annulled policy. However, the prime minister successfully presided over the irrigation venture known as the Helmand Valley Project, which created a closer relationship with the United States, especially after the country provided much of the financial backing for the effort.

In 1947, the Durand Line would once again surface as an issue with the government of Afghanistan. At the first implementation of the Pashtunistan demarcation line in 1893, the reigning Amir Abdur Rahman felt anger and resentment over the terms of the agreement with the British, often complaining how he had been forced into signing the agreement. This notion still carried through several decades in the Afghan government, even in light of the years of cooperation and diplomacy with the British. Gradually over time, the Durand Line became a point of contention between the political regimes of Afghanistan and Pakistan and the Pashtun tribesmen caught in the middle. Complicating the situation further with India was a new British policy in the North-West Frontier Province.[7] As part of this policy, the Muslims of the region were forced to choose between the Hindu-dominated state of India or the Muslim population of Pakistan. In July 1947, the Pashtun inhabitants in the North-West Frontier Province overwhelmingly elected to be part of Pakistan. Further, the Tribal Agencies held a loya jirga, and once again the tribes chose allegiance to Pakistan. Afghanistan accepted the decision with diplomacy, but the matter continued to remain unresolved until 1949, when a Pakistani air force plane bombed a local Pashtun village. In light of these new events, Afghanistan took a firm stance in a loya jirga, deciding that the artificial Durand Line (and any similar line) was invalid and, furthermore, that all agreements and treaties regarding the issue since 1893 would not be recognized by Afghanistan. Relations between the governments of Pakistan and Afghanistan suffered, and as a consequence, Pakistan ceased the transport of a petroleum shipment into Afghanistan in 1950 and held the cargo for three months in an act of defiance. The incident forced the hand of the Afghan government to sign a treaty with the Soviet Union several months later in July 1950. The agreement involved the amicable trade of Soviet commodities, such as oil and textiles, in exchange for Afghan wool and cotton. The Soviets also offered aid in several construction efforts in Afghanistan, such as petroleum storage facilities. In addition, as a further benefit to the Afghan economy, the agreement offered the free transportation of goods across Soviet territory. As such, Prime Minister Shah Mahmud's efforts during the Pashtunistan issue and the Soviet agreement would have a profound impact on the political aspirations and liberalization of Afghanistan. Not only did this agreement benefit Afghanistan by providing an viable alternative to the Pakistan blockage of trade, which had severely disrupted the economy of Afghanistan, but the agreement with the Soviets also robustly increased interaction and technological advancements in Afghanistan.

THE LIBERAL PARLIAMENT OF 1949

After World War II, Afghanistan began to exhibit an outlook of political open-mindedness, freedom, and liberalization. This newly developed sphere of tolerance had been highly advanced by the emergence and support of the Western style of thinking. The influential political leaders garnered support for the prime minister to hold less controlled elections for the National Assembly, thus leading to the first "liberal parliament." As such, Prime Minister Sardar Shah Mahmud recognized the importance of diverse political groups to represent the spectrum of political interests in Afghanistan, and many of these groups supported a more open political system. These groups contributed to such social acts as conducting debates, producing theatrical plays on subjects such as the monarchy or the role of Islam in Afghanistan, and publishing newspaper articles.

Unfortunately, the multitude of diverse groups emerged in rapid succession and ultimately overwhelmed the prime minister, who tried, in vain, to counter this effort by forming his own overarching political party. After his unsuccessful attempts to do so, the prime minister determined that since his own party was not worthy enough, then none of the other groups would be either. As such, in 1951, he terminated all the previously created political groups and eliminated the amount of political liberalization. The student union in Kabul was closed, and newspapers that once were valued for free speech regarding government plans and political themes were shut down. The following year, the elected parliament represented a dramatic difference from the liberal assembly that had been elected three years previously. After the new parliamentary election, the brief period of liberalism in Afghanistan was over. The government cleanup of political tolerance in 1951 alienated many young Afghanis who were trying to improve the political structure for the benefit of the country and not, as the government believed, to create a radically different stance and insurgence in Afghanistan.

PRIME MINISTER DAOUD AND THE URBANIZATION OF AFGHANISTAN: 1953

The failed political and liberalization reforms in the early 1950s created a rift in the royal Afghan house and began to challenge the control held by the king's uncles. Mohammad Daoud Khan became prime minister in September 1953, and Daoud was both the cousin of the king and his brother-in-law. The placement of Daoud as prime minister was a public recognition of the royal family's attempts at embracing Western thought, for Daoud was the first Western-educated member of the royal family to hold a position of power. Daoud's main concern as prime minister was to eradicate the Afghan government's stance and bias on the Western way of thought. Daoud's would continue to support the Helmand Project as begun under his predecessor, Prime Minister Sardar Shah Mahmud Khan. To further his stance on modernism and in conjunction with the Durand Line ramifications, Daoud sought to expand relations with the Soviet Union and continued to distance himself Pakistan.

In the 30 years since the dawn of reformation under King Amanullah, Afghanistan was still trying to transform out of its antiquated doldrums into a more modern society. Prime Minister Daoud also supported the emancipation of the women of Afghanistan, including social advancements for women, once again leading the effort to end the requirement for women to wear veiled coverings in public.[8] In 1959 as Afghanistan was preparing to celebrate its 40th year of independence, Daoud also invited the wives of his ministers to join in the celebration without the typical veiled attire. Religious leaders vehemently protested this so-called shameful request, and Daoud challenged their objections by requesting these conventional leaders to show him the verse in the Qur'an that mandates that women be veiled. When these religious leaders could not find the reference but continued to object to Daoud's request, they were thrown into jail.

RELATIONS WITH THE SOVIET UNION

Prime Minister Daoud achieved some success in his reforms of foreign policy, but these reforms created economic instability in the country. His goals in foreign policy were to improve relations with the Soviet Union without harming economic aid from the United States and also to pursue and resolve the Pashtunian issue, which would consume him throughout his career. Because of the increasingly hostile relations encouraged by Pakistan, the economic trade of Afghanistan began to suffer. Afghanistan had little choice as a landlocked country with no access to an independent port, and furthermore the country could no longer interact on cordial terms with Pakistan. For these reasons, Afghanistan was forced to ally with the Soviet Union. However, Daoud recognized that Afghanistan needed to consider other avenues, and thus he sought to expand foreign policy for aid and assistance from the other superpowers in the world.

To further intensify the already strained situation, the border between Afghanistan and Pakistan was closed for five months in 1955, and both Iran and the United States were unable to create another viable trade route for Afghanistan. Prime Minister Daoud's desire for improved relations became imperative with the Soviet Union, and to help achieve this objective, the treaty established in 1950 would be amended and ratified again in June 1955 to allow the transit of bartered goods. In an effort to renew the treaty and secure an amicable partnership, Soviet President Nikita Khruschev visited Kabul, and the Soviet-Afghan relationship was once again renewed. This also included a US$100 million development loan for mutual Afghan-Soviet projects.

Despite the escalation of the Cold War between the United States and the Soviet Union, Afghanistan continued to engage in trade and to expand relations with both countries. Over the years, the United States had become more interested in the countries known as the "Northern Tier," which included Iran, Iraq, Pakistan, Turkey, and, most notably, Afghanistan. The United States diligently worked to foster an allegiance agreement with the government, but Prime Minister Daoud continued the traditional stance of nonpartisan politics. Despite the continuous encouragement from the United States, Afghanistan refused to join the Baghdad Pact with Iraq, Turkey, and Iran as mandated by the United States and Great Britain. The agreement was part of the superpowers anticommunist regime against the Soviet Union, and it is largely speculated Afghanistan's nonconcurrence was due to a lack of guaranteed protection for Afghanistan in the case of a retaliatory Soviet attack with no political infringement from these superpowers. As a result, the United States would not provide Afghanistan with any military assistance.[9] Once again, Afghanistan turned to its allies the Soviets to provide support, and Daoud received more than $25 million in military aid and supplies. Likewise, the Soviets also began to build several military airfields in Mazari Sharif, Bagram, and Shindand.

STRAIN WITH PAKISTAN: THE PASHTUNIAN ISSUE

The Pashtunian issue was the second topic of greatest concern to Prime Minister Daoud and would continue to consume his efforts to the point that no other issues mattered more than the Pashtunian resolution. Previously, throughout the early 1950s, Daoud offered payments to the Pashtun tribesman in a dual effort to destabilize the government and policy of Pakistan while also increasing the distribution of propaganda. The situation heightened in 1955 when Pakistan abolished the four governments of West Pakistan and formed one conjoined unit despite the Afghan government's protest. The Pakistan–Afghan border would close in the spring of 1955, which severed the ability for trade transit and increased the Afghan need for relations with the Soviet Union. The Pashtunian issue would continue for several more years, and relations improved only slightly between the two countries. In 1960, Daoud ordered Afghan forces into Pakistan in an endeavor to finally subdue the Pashtunian issue once and for all, and throughout the effort, propaganda was relentlessly played on the radio. On September 6, 1961, relations between the two countries were completely severed when Pakistan immediately ceased all transit, both for imports and exports. One such shipment was a crop export of grapes and pomegranates bound for India, which the Soviets graciously offered to purchase and transport via aircraft from Afghanistan. The United States made attempts to arbitrate the dispute between Pakistan and Afghanistan, but Pakistan continued to hold supplies, some of which were meant for development projects in Afghanistan. As a result, the economy continued to decline because of the lack of income from trade revenue and foreign exchange.

As a further impediment to any form of resolution, Pakistan closed the border to the seasonal travelers that frequently crossed the border to spend winters in Pakistan and summers in Afghanistan. By 1963, it was abundantly clear that neither country would acquiesce on the situation. Both Prime Minister Daoud of Afghanistan and Ayub Khan of Pakistan were resolute in their own stance, and the only option for progress was to remove one of these men from power. While both men were strong in their own positions, for each had attained both praise and criticism during their tenure in office, the weakened economy in Afghanistan would lead to the downfall for Daoud as prime minister. Consequently, King Zahir Shah asked for Daoud's resignation based on the depleting economy that was the result of both his incessant perseverance and his lack of resolution to the Pashtunian issue. With no other option after the dispute in Pakistan resulted in an economic crisis for the country, Daoud was asked to resign in 1963.[10] On Daoud's resignation, Muhammad Yousuf became prime minister, a non-Pashtun whose limited experience previously included being the minister of mines and industries.

THE LAST DECADE OF MONARCHY IN AFGHANISTAN: 1963–1973

King Zahir, during this final decade of his rule, was free from the influence of his uncles and relatives, and he began to take a more active stance in the affairs of his country. Independent from outside control and free to experiment with democracy, in 1964 King Zahir championed the need for a liberal constitution that provided a bicameral legislature. As part of this legislature, the representatives would be appointed in a ratio of one-third each by the king, the provincial assemblies, and the Afghan people.

The replacement of Daoud Khan resulted in swift change in diplomatic and trade relations with Pakistan. Issues that were once pushed aside by Daoud were finally able to be resolved. Within weeks of Daoud's resignation, the king designated a new council to outline and plan a new charter for Afghanistan. As such, the greatest achievement of this era would be the resolution of the 1964 Constitution. Earlier in the year, King Zahir ordered a loya jirga that required members of the National Assembly, the Senate, the Supreme Court, and the constitutional board to convene with the intention of electing new representatives. At the loya jirga, new representatives were elected or appointed by the king, and in September 1964 the constitutional assembly included 452 representatives from the country, six of whom were women. All

452 members signed the new Constitution on September 20, and King Zahir officially ratified the document 10 days later.

The signing of the Constitution of 1964 marked a historically significant moment in the formation of the nation. Primarily, the multiple steps required in the involvement, planning, and drafting of the Constitution ultimately represented changes that had been made in traditional political thinking. The championing of individual rights and freedoms by provincial delegates rather than tribal chiefs demonstrated the movement of Afghanistan from a tribal society into the contemporary era, a dream that was begun under Ahmad Durrani in 1747 for tribal autonomy. Further, the iconic backbone and belief in the Muslim faith had existed in Afghanistan since A.D. 652 and was affirmed by establishing Islam as the national religion in Afghanistan. Similarly, the Constitution also stated that the word *Afghan* would henceforth denote all citizens of the nation and no longer only those of Pashtun origin. By implementing such measures as the freedom of press, assembly, and association, the Constitution supported new developments in the country and furthered the women's movement by increasing their involvement in political parties and the fight for equal rights. In addition, the Constitution established an independent judiciary system that was unconstrained by the previous legal system, which was based on religion and obviously favored by religious leaders. Recognizing the importance and need to enact an unbiased and fair system, the Constitution implemented the supremacy of secular law. Furthermore, the government of Afghanistan would now be a constitutional monarchy (rather than an absolute monarchy) with a bicameral legislature and elected parliament, which allowed the majority of power to remain with the king.[11] The Wolasi Jirga (House of Representatives) would be known as the lower house of parliament and be composed of 216 members from both ends of the political spectrum. King Zahir also nominated a new prime minister, Mohammad Hashim Maiwandwal.

The new freedom reforms in the Constitution resulted in the development of extremist political parties, such as the communist-based People's Democratic Party of Afghanistan (PDPA) on January 1, 1965. The PDPA was well known to have strong ties to the Soviet Union and was established with the intention of gaining more seats in the parliament. The leftist party successfully achieved this goal, and four PDPA members were elected. One such elected official, Nur Muhammad Taraki, established the first major radical newspaper in Afghanistan known as *The Khalq*, which endured for only one month before being shut down by the government for the extremist literature it supported.

In 1967, the PDPA split into several different sects, the most prominent two being the Khalq (Masses) faction led by Taraki and the Parcham (Banner) faction led by Babrak Karmal. The schism would serve to reflect the divisions of ethnicity, class, and ideology within Afghan society. As such, the Khalq supporters were mainly Pashtuns from rural Afghanistan who embodied the Khalq belief in supporting the working class. The Parcham sect was composed of the more urban citizens in Afghanistan who supported the socioeconomic democratic front. While both divisions were regarded as extreme, the king tolerated the Parcham and was more lenient of their publications than that of the Khalq. Karmal was allowed to publish his newspaper, *Parcham*, from March 1968 to July 1969 while King Zahir officially banned the Khalq newspaper, leading to accusations of Parcham having a hidden association with the king.[12]

The 1969 elections resulted in the loss of many incumbent seats, including those held by all six women in parliament. Further, a large number of non-Pashtun members were elected, and the new parliament now represented more landowners and businessmen than the previous administration in 1965. As a final blow, the Prime Minister Maiwandwal lost his seat as a Democratic Socialist. As a result of the new election, the next four years left Afghan politics in instability and volatility, as the incongruent political representation in the parliament often resulted in an impasse on any form of progress. Until 1973, the public's outcry of dissatisfaction with the government prompted a clear division with political representation on both ends of the political spectrum. Toward the end of his reign, King Zahir became increasingly criticized for the lack of support he gave to his prime ministers. As this internal dissatisfaction, coupled with the political polarization in Afghanistan, continued to heighten, a seemingly silent and long-forgotten usurper lay in waiting in the shadows. This chaotic ambiance gave Daoud the opportunity he had been desperately waiting for since he was forced to resign 10 years earlier.

MOHAMMAD SARDAR DAOUD KHAN AND THE CREATION OF THE REPUBLIC OF AFGHANISTAN: 1973–1978

In the early 1970s, Afghanistan was on the brink of crisis. A severe drought devastated the crops, and as a result Afghanistan's economy spiraled downward. The government faced charges of corruption, and while the king was out of the country for medical treatment, Daoud seized control in a nearly bloodless coup.[13] The stability that King Zahir had strived for under his "New Democracy" was not achieved, and in one swift move the rule of the monarchy as begun by Ahmad Shah Durrani in 1747 was abolished.

On July 17, 1973, it was under these circumstances that Prime Minister Daoud seized power via a military coup and forced the shah to exile in Italy. The rebellious coup had been planned for more than a year and was aided by junior officers in the Soviet Union. Further support came from those whom Daoud ironically referred to as his "friends," including factions of Barbrak

Karmal's Parcham Party. Daoud's reemergence in Afghanistan was generally favored, and Daoud promptly abolished monarchical rule in Afghanistan and simultaneously eradicated the 1964 Constitution. He additionally stated that Afghanistan would now be a republican government with himself as the first president. He reinstated his previous regime, which focused on the Pashtunian issue, still an important topic to conservative Pashtun officers. Previously as prime minister, Daoud had received modern weapons from the Soviet Union, and his experience as a former military officer left him in good standing with the military. In 1976, Daoud established his own political party, the National Revolutionist Party, which would be the nucleus of all political interests. The following year in a loya jirga, the new Constitution established by Daoud implemented a presidential system of government.

Over his five-year tenure as president of Afghanistan, Daoud's relationship with the Soviet Union and internal Afghan communists deteriorated gradually, beginning in 1974. This was partly due to Daoud's shift to the right side of the political spectrum and his aligning Afghanistan away from communism. However, Afghanistan continued to side with the Soviets throughout representational voting in the United Nations. Without question, the Soviets had been the chief provider of assistance and support for Afghanistan, and as such the country was highly influential in the economic, political, and social interaction with other countries. Daoud still pushed his state-centered economic strategy in his seven-year plan from 1976 to 1983, which, in order to succeed, would require a great deal of foreign aid. Since Daoud had shifted away from accepting economic and military support from the Soviets, Afghanistan sought to build relationships with other countries. Daoud recognized that any unity with other countries must have the power and strength, both economically and politically, to assist Afghanistan if it was going to completely break ties with the Soviet Union. As such, Daoud turned to several nations for assistance, including the oil-rich countries Saudi Arabia, Iraq, and Kuwait, to provide financial backing; to India for increased military support; and to Iran for assistance in economic development. However, relations with Pakistan improved by 1977 with the aid of the United States, and in March 1978, President Daoud visited Islamabad. The intention of the meeting was to negotiate an agreement with President Muhammad Zia-ul-Haq of for a prisoner exchange and also to agree to the expulsion of Pashtun and Baloch militants from Afghanistan. The meeting proved successful, and relations with Pakistan gradually improved. By the spring of 1978, Daoud had achieved little of what he had originally planned five years before. While there was some economic progress, the standard of living in Afghanistan had not improved, and as a result Daoud was alienated from many political groups. Furthermore, the conservative Pashtunian supporters still resented Daoud's agreement with Pakistan on the Pashtun militants in Afghanistan.

THE APRIL 1978 COUP

Daoud's attempts to renovate and improve the government by implementing economic and social reforms would not be successful, and the new Constitution in February 1977 did nothing to stabilize the political volatility of the country. This mayhem resulted in action from the extremist political party of the formerly banned leftist party of the PDPA. With the political, economic, and social structure in Afghanistan turned upside down, the PDPA successfully implemented and carried out a bloody coup on April 27, 1978.

Daoud feared the rebelliousness pulsing through the communist veins of the country. After the assassination of Mir Akbar Khayber, a member of the PDPA, the funeral served as a gathering place for the Afghan communists, with an estimated 30,000 persons gathering to hear speeches by the communist leaders Nur Mohammed Taraki and Babrak Karmal. Appalled at this collective demonstration and shocked by the striking unity of the crowd, Daoud ordered the arrest of these PDPA leaders, but he did not direct this soon enough because of his misconception that Parcham was the more immediate threat. For more than a week, the PDPA leaders escaped punishment until Taraki was arrested and Hafizullah Amin placed under house arrest, allowing him time to detail the plans for the coup from home while using his family as messengers.[14] On April 27, 1978, the coup began with troops and tanks moving into Kabul International Airport. Insurgent units formed around the capital, and over the course of the day, the number of rebel units steadily increased throughout the city. Within 24 hours, President Daoud and his family were killed in the Presidential Palace. These plans were successfully executed while all the civilian leaders of the PDPA were imprisoned, and the coup ended the republican rule begun by Ahmad Shah Durrani more than 230 years earlier. Now under control of the communist regime, Nur Muhammad Taraki became president of the Revolutionary Council and prime minister of the Soviet-supported Democratic Republic of Afghanistan.

NOTES

1. Senzil Nawid, *Religious Response to Social Change in Afghanistan 1919–29.* Several members of the Young Afghans were arrested in an attempt to murder King Habibollah with the intention of replacing him with his modern-thinking son. However, the plan was uncovered, and the king's own son Amanullah was named among the conspirators. Amanullah escaped severe punishment because of the intervention of his Uncle Nasrullah, but obviously the incident created a bitter sentiment, and he was banished from the king's favor. With their plan defeated, the Young Afghans became more frustrated and instituted Prince Amanullah since he embodied their beliefs in nationalism and independence from foreign occupation.

2. Oliver Roy, *Islam and Resistance in Afghanistan.* As perceived by King Amanullah, Afghanistan was a devout Muslim state that was created by the infidels of Britain and Russia.

3. Nawid, *Religious Response to Social Change in Afghanistan 1919–29.* This is the first assault by aircraft in the history of Afghanistan, and afterward, King Amanullah negotiated with the Soviets for his own aerial force.

4. Stephen Tanner, *Afghanistan: A Military History from Alexander the Great to the Fall of the Taliban.* As part of the Afghan resentment in devising the Durand Line, Sir Mortimer Durand created the artificial line in such a crooked manner that the line even divided a farmer's house from his field.

5. Jules Stewart, *The Khyber Rifles: From the British Raj to Al Qaeda.*

6. Bernard Lewis, *The Middle East: A Brief History of the Last 2,000 Years.* As the founder of the Turkish Republic, Ataturk was also the first president. King Amanullah was deeply impressed with Ataturk's reforms of Turkey and sought to implement such factions in Afghanistan.

7. The North-West Frontier Province was established on November 9, 1901.

8. However, Islamic fundamentalists who were not in favor of these urban reforms took matters into their own hands. This period in time marks the first instance of men throwing acid onto the faces of unveiled women, thus hoping that the disfigurement would force the women to cover their faces out of embarrassment. However, these extreme measures would not dissuade these early female pioneers, and a multitude of women bravely defended their freedom by walking out in public without veiled faces. These vicious acts would gain more publicity some 50 years later when the Taliban assumed control of Afghanistan and corroborated the custom of defacing women with acid.

9. Martin Ewans, *Afghanistan: A Short History of Its People and Politics.* The pact later became known as the Central Treaty Organization (CENTO), which was the term used after Iraq left the agreement in 1959.

10. Ewans, *Afghanistan.* Also cited during this period, the Afghan prison system had been investigated for its appalling conditions, as previously ignored by Daoud.

11. Abdul G. Farahi, *Afghanistan during Democracy and Republic: 1963–1978.* The author provides a copious amount of detail during the setup of the 1964 Constitution and the assemblies thereafter.

12. Roy, *Islam and Resistance in Afghanistan.* Partly resentful and partly suspicious over Daoud's tolerance of Parcham, the political party of Khalq propagated Parcham as the Royal Communist Party.

13. The king was in Italy receiving eye treatment at the medicinal mud baths in Ischia.

14. Ewans, *Afghanistan.* The organization and execution of the coup was so well planned that many believe that Soviet officials, the KGB, or the Central Intelligence Agency had to have assisted the Khalq.

8

The Soviet Invasion and the Afghan Civil War, 1979–1992

The Soviet invasion officially began with the deployment of the 40th Army into Kabul Airport on December 25, 1979, and would last until the Soviets began their troop withdrawal on May 15, 1988 with the last of the Soviet forces leaving in February 1989. Over the duration of nearly 10 years, the conflict resulted from the Soviets' support of the Marxist-based People's Democratic Party of Afghanistan (PDPA) against the rebel forces of the mujahideen. Specifically, the term *mujahideen* refers to a group of Afghan insurgents who fought to overthrow the communist rule of Afghanistan and were assisted by such countries as the United States, Great Britain, and China. The mujahideen received additional support from other Muslim countries, such as Pakistan, Saudi Arabia, Iran, Egypt, and Jordan. The mujahideen rebels received support from these nations not only to champion Afghanistan's freedom from communist rule but also as a primary effort to stop the Cold War aggression into the Persian Gulf. By the middle of the 1980s, the Afghan resistance movement had received a substantial amount of aid by these countries, and the Afghan fighters had been trained extensively by the United States and Pakistan as part of the Cold War struggle. Referred to as Operation Cyclone, the U.S. Central Intelligence Agency (CIA) provided assistance in defeating these communist forces through the Pakistani Inter-Services Intelligence (ISI), the largest and most powerful of the three intelligence services in Pakistan.[1] The

ISI was formed for intelligence gathering and the training of spies in addition to supporting Pakistan's nuclear program and ensuring the security of Pakistan's top army generals. The Soviet invasion of Afghanistan resulted in a humiliating defeat for the Soviets, and the war is often referred to as the Soviet Union's Vietnam.

KHALQ CONTROL: 1978–1980

After the overthrow of 200 years of democracy in Afghanistan on April 28, 1978, the country was now under the control of the veiled communist regime of the PDPA. After the assassination of President Daoud, Nur Muhammad Taraki assumed the threefold role of president of the Revolutionary Council, prime minister, and general secretary of the Soviet-supported Democratic Republic of Afghanistan (DRA). The PDPA government structure was divided along partisan lines, including the Khalq faction led by Muhammad Taraki and Hafizullah Amin against the Parcham leaders of Babrak Karmal and Mohammad Najibullah. When the PDPA began their rule of Afghanistan, many citizens were unaware of the existence of the Khalq Party, and the party fostered further confusion of its identity by not declaring that the party was under the control of the communist regime. Shrouded in obscurity at first, Khalq propaganda used words such as *democratic* and *nationalist*. Although the party line was not forthcoming in stating that it was under communist rule, this was widely believed to be the case. As such, the United States was apprehensive to provide support at first since, although Afghanistan was not a communist country yet, the Foreign Assistance Act prohibited assistance to any foreign countries that were under communist control. In May 1978, Afghanistan signed an agreement with Soviet forces to provide nearly 400 military advisers for the Afghan army, a decision that would eventually cripple the Afghan forces when the Soviets invaded 18 months later.

The PDPA was founded in 1965 by Mohammad Taraki, Babrak Karmal, and Hafizullah Amin on deeply implemented Marxist ideals that were flowing through the policies trying to be implemented in Afghanistan. The goal of the Khalq Party was to completely reform Afghanistan under a socialist agenda— if not willingly, then by force. The internal struggle between the Khalq and the Parcham parties led to the banishment of Babrak Kamal and furthermore led to the arrest and execution of many Parchami supporters, including members of the Afghan elite, religious associates, and community intelligentsia. In October 1978, the communist mask of the Khalq regime would be thrown to the ground at the unveiling of the new flag of Afghanistan. The Khalq revealed the new flag at a rally in Kabul, one that would no longer be primarily green and white but, rather, covered in crimson red. The flag was almost a replica of other communist flags, and after the rally the it became clear that the future of Afghanistan had been declared communist under the Khalq control. Furthering communist alliances in December 1978, the Khalq signed an amicable partnership with the Soviet Union to permit the deployment of Soviet military assistance at the request of the Afghan government. These actions committed the country to the Soviet communist regime, and these policy implementation efforts eventually instigated the Soviet invasion.[2] Through the requested alliances and the agreements for Soviet support to modernize the economic infrastructure of Afghanistan, the PDPA regime had become increasingly reliant on Soviet assistance and depended on the Soviets for military support and advisers. The new Afghan government under the DRA looked to the Soviets for economic assistance to build roads, mine natural resources, and train the Afghan army.

The Khalq grew increasingly stronger with men like Taraki and Amin at the forefront, and the Khalq issued various economic and social decrees as part of their Marxist policies. Furthermore, the objective of the Khalq was to destroy the frontier power structures and educate the peasants so that they would support the Khalq. While at first these measures sounded noble, they did not take into account the customs of Afghan social structure or formation, and as a result these reforms deeply offended the tribal and family structures in Afghanistan. These measures included the radical concept of instituting educational requirements for both men and women. Additional reforms included the establishment of marriage rules, which included bridal choice by banning not only forced marriages but also the minimum age of marrying and ceasing *mehr*, the requirement for a bridal dowry to be paid. These reforms also included land restructuring measures to spread the distribution of land among the poor residents of Afghanistan, and in doing so, these methods both reduced the landholding requirements in Afghanistan and eliminated usury, the charging of outrageous sums of interests on Afghan loans.[3] However, the land reforms were instituted swiftly and without documentation or accuracy, and as a result many were discouraged by the confusion in the banking and legal systems. Furthermore, the land reform measures undermined the Afghan system and its foundation. The difficulty increased with further additions to the education reforms and with the establishment of a national language for the Nuristani, Uzbek, Turkmen, and Baluchi ethnic clans. Traditional religious laws had been replaced by Marxist rules, and once these reforms joined with the liberation and education efforts for women, these Khalq regimes were perceived as an attack against Islam.

The backlash was forthcoming against the monopolistic rule of the PDPA, and consequently revolts emerged everywhere in Afghanistan. The rebellions against these reforms were often violent and often increased into all-out tribal attacks. In October, the Nuristani tribe in the Kunar valley rebelled, and this initial rebellion inspired other ethnic revolts. Those who tried to oppose the

Khalq communist regime were severely punished, and more often than not, these traitors were executed. The Khalq scoured the countryside for such infidels under a sweeping reign of terror, and these traitors included not only Afghan professionals but also military officials, religious figures, and former political leaders. Prison conditions were the most extreme at Pul-i-Charki, an infamous prison located on the outskirts of Kabul. The prison was not even completed, yet it was used to accommodate prisoners and offenders against the DRA, most often until these detainees were executed for their actions. Nearly six months after the Daoud coup in the fall of 1978, Amnesty International estimated there were as many as 4,000 prisoners held in the prison, and the following year the estimate had tripled to 12,000 who were detained without trial. In the 18 months between the Daoud coup in April 1978 and the Soviet invasion in December 1979, as many as 27,000 prisoners were executed at Pul-i-Charki.[4] Most of these prisoners were taken without their families even knowing where their loved ones had gone and for the most part were left to wonder if these family members were still alive or had already been killed.

In February 1979, the American involvement in the overthrow escalated when the U.S. ambassador to Kabul, Adolph Dubs, was captured by four members of a leftist group and held hostage. Soviet counsels and advisers guided the Afghan leaders in the resolution of the conflict, and as such the Soviets refused to negotiate with Dubs's captors and ultimately decided to storm the room without consulting with the United States. Unfortunately, the situation resulted in the death not only of Dubs's captors but of the hostage Dubs himself. The lack of concurrence from the United States prompted an immediate withdrawal and denial of additional support to Afghanistan. Many accounts place the blame for the incident among several individuals, with implications that the culprits were the Parcham, which was trying to bring revenge on the Khalq. In another allegation, the Soviets alleged that the Dubs plot was the result of the CIA trying to further intensify the situation and discredit the Khalq regime.[5] Nonetheless, with both sides pointing fingers and devising allegations, Hafizullah Amin had gained considerable control and replaced Taraki as prime minister. The situation in Afghanistan was intensifying at an alarming rate, and without U.S.-sanctioned support, the Afghan civilians did not have a viable government structure to hear their outrage. With no other alternative to express frustration and anger over the circumstances, the Afghans stormed Herat in a rebellious force and ruthlessly slaughtered Soviet forces. After a month, the rebellion was finally put down, but not before the Afghans had killed more than 100 Soviets advisers and their families and paraded their severed heads on crude spikes through the streets of Herat. Over the next several months, the tribal revolts increased and spread like wildfire throughout Afghanistan. However, the Khalq assembly continued to insist that these reform measures were being accepted and put into action with great success. On the contrary, these false claims were a vain attempt to hide the dissension that was brewing within Afghanistan. Once this was brought out into the open, Khalq blamed the foreign saboteurs for the unsuccessful land reform measures, and by the spring of 1979, more than 85 percent of the provinces in Afghanistan had revolted against the Khalq regime.[6]

Soviet President Leonid Brezhnev met with Taraki to discuss the situation, and during this meeting the two agreed that Amin had gained too much control and influence and that the only solution was to remove Amin from power. On his return to Kabul, Taraki requested a meeting with Amin, but Amin would attend only on the condition that he would be safe from Soviet harm. As such, Amin requested Soviet Ambassador Alexander Puzanov to guarantee his safety. Perhaps the agreement for protection was too hasty, for despite the agreed-on request, Amin was now highly suspicious of Taraki, deducing the possibility of an assassination attempt and figuring that the guaranteed protection request of the Soviet ambassador was mere lip service. Amin figured that if Taraki would agree to such a stipulation so quickly, then something certainly was going to occur. On his arrival at the Presidential Palace, a shoot-out occurred, and Amin escaped briefly, only to return shortly with his supporters to take Taraki hostage. By the middle of September 1979, Amin announced his control of the government. However, records are not clear whether Taraki was killed during the gunfight or taken as hostage and later killed. However, on September 16, Amin announced that he had to replace Taraki for medical reasons, and in early October, Amin declared that Taraki had died of an unknown illness.[7] Since Amin was in complete opposition with the Soviets, the situation was further complicated when Amin demanded that the Soviets withdraw Ambassador Puzanov from Afghanistan. In addition, Amin knew the Soviets had already attempted to kill him and were continuing efforts to eliminate him from power. As such Amin worked to garner much-needed support and he tried to make amends for situations in Afghanistan. Throughout October and November, Amin tried desperately to gather allies to protect him and he attempted to open communications with Pakistan. He looked internally into his own country to make reparations through his attempts to implement a new constitution and also his offer of amnesty to refugees to return to the country. While hastily trying to implement these rebuilding efforts, Amin drafted a list of some 12,000 prisoners who had been killed in prison since the Saur Revolution. For many families in Afghanistan, husbands and young sons had been wrongfully imprisoned, and more often than not, their family did not know what happened to them. Amin intended to console these families by officially recognizing that these prisoners had been executed, and he released this list to the public. However, the execution list angered the Afghan citizens and resulted in a backlash because the list proved the atrociousness of the government. By December, the situation in

Afghanistan was critical, with an internal revolt rising against Amin and the Soviets on the brink of invasion.

THE SOVIET INVASION AND OCCUPATION: 1979–1988

The irony of the nine-year Soviet occupation is that the Afghan government specifically requested the Soviet forces to come to Afghanistan for support against rebel forces. Under the backlash of the PDPA, many rebel groups formed to eradicate the Soviet dependency in Afghanistan, and these groups were gaining momentum. As such, throughout 1979, Babrak Kamal requested several times for Soviet assistance to provide security against the mujahideen rebellions. Some accounts allege that Hafizullah Amin also had requested Soviet troops and support, although evidence shows that Amin stated on several occasions in 1979 that he had no need for Soviet assistance.[8] The Soviet government in Moscow desperately wanted to remove Hafizullah Amin and replace him with Babrak Karmal, and the Soviets realized that this could not be achieved by only aerial assault and that ground troops would be necessary as well. By early December, the Soviets had placed forces around Kabul Airport and at the air base at Bagram. The Soviets entered Afghanistan with multiple rifle and airborne divisions and marched into the frontier provinces. By the middle of December, American intelligence sources clearly were aware of the advancing Soviet troops into Afghanistan. By the late evening of December 24, Soviet planes began to land continuously at Kabul Airport, and by December 27, the Soviets had successfully infiltrated multiple battalions with enough military force to attack the city.

Previously, Soviet advisers successfully disengaged Afghan troops by using such tactics as removing batteries from tanks, citing "maintenance reasons"; removing live rounds from weapons and replacing them with blanks as part of "training exercises"; and further imprisoning senior officers for miscellaneous petty offenses. In addition, the Soviets had previously dismantled the Afghan communication systems, and by implementing these strategic ploys, the Soviets were free to march into the country with tanks, troops, and weapons against a force of improperly equipped Afghan soldiers with virtually no armored vehicles, no firepower, and no military leaders. Against a practically paralyzed Afghan army, sometime during the night of December 27, some of the Soviet troops took over the city and stormed the Presidential Palace, killing Amin and his family. However, within several days, Karmal had announced via broadcast over Radio Kabul that Amin had been overthrown and that Karmal was now the president of Afghanistan. By January 1, 1980, more than 50,000 Soviet troops and 1,000 military vehicles had been deployed into Afghanistan, and over the next month the Soviet troops increased to 85,000. Simultaneously, an increasing number of Afghan troops were deserting because of low morale brought on by their inability to subdue the revolting tribes, with numbers depleting from 90,000 troops to an unreliable force of only 30,000 by 1980.[9]

The world reacted strongly to the invasion, and the United States under President Jimmy Carter declared that the Soviet undertaking was a threat to world peace and, further, that the onslaught into Afghanistan was regarded as the most dangerous menace in the world since World War II. The Soviets countered by devising allegations and reasons to distract from the root of the cause, even to the point that the Soviets attempted to explain the invasion by arguing that Hafizullah Amin had been a spy for America. When pressed further, the Soviets were unable to provide any factual evidence to support these allegations. The United States instated severe measures, including the restriction of a shipment of 17 tons of grain into the Soviet Union, the immediate cessation of Soviet fishing in American waters, a broadcast to boycott the 1980 Moscow Olympics, and the announced delay of the second sanction of the Strategic Arms Limitation Talks (SALT). The SALT deliberations concerned the issue of armaments control and were composed of two separate panels of bilateral discussions during the Cold War between the United States and the Soviet Union. The discussions consisted of two parts—referred to as SALT I from 1969 to 1972 and SALT II from 1972 to 1979—and the U.S. Senate delayed the SALT II Treaty. The treaty became known as the Strategic Arms Reduction Treaty (START) and was signed between President Brezhnev and President Carter in Vienna, Austria, on June 18, 1979. However, because of the Soviet invasion of Afghanistan, the U.S. Senate never ratified the treaty, though the terms of the treaty were still honored by both the Soviet Union and the United States. In addition, the U.S. government embraced the so-called Carter Doctrine in an attempt to prevent any Soviet aggression and hegemony into the Persian Gulf. President Carter announced the doctrine in his State of the Union Address on January 23, 1980, stipulating that the United States had vital interests in the Persian Gulf and that any invasion would result in the use of immediate force if necessary to protect national interests. In the meantime, the Soviet forces in Afghanistan had grown substantially.

Furthermore, the refugee situation had grown progressively worse. Previously, by the end of 1979, Pakistan had accepted nearly 80,000 refugees in the country, and already by the time of the Soviet invasion, resistance groups had formed and were preparing small skirmishes into Afghanistan. The following year, as many as 750,000 refugees had moved into Pakistan and more than 100,000 into Iran. By 1981, the number of refugees had doubled in Pakistan, and by 1984 the numbers were shocking: a total of nearly 4 million in Pakistan and almost 2 million in Iran. The numbers would continue to grow until more than 6 million Afghan citizens had fled the country, with estimates of another nearly 2 million seeking sanctuary inside the country as internal refugees. The United States provided financial support to Pakistan for the Afghan refugees and also for the multitude of problems that crossed the border with them. Along with the arrival of the Afghan refugees came a sharp increase in drugs and weapons, and the large influx of so many refugees had a profound effect on Pakistan economically, socially, and politically.

As part of the backlash against the communist regime and Soviet occupation, many rebel groups formed in an attempt to sabotage and destroy some aspects of the Soviet regime. As such, the mujahideen resistance in Afghanistan was formed, made up of Islamic warrior forces who fought against the Soviet invasion. The United States secretly provided arms to the mujahideen forces, and the CIA provided funding for these efforts via the American taxpayers. Throughout the nine-year Soviet occupation, these Afghan rebels and religious zealots were significantly financed, armed, and trained by the CIA beginning with the presidency of Jimmy Carter and continuing under Ronald Reagan, who famously praised the multitude of mujahideen rebels as "freedom fighters." Several other countries contributed support to the mujahideen against the Soviet army, including Saudi Arabia, China, Iran, and also Pakistan under the ISI. While the CIA may have provided the funding for the weapons against the Soviets, the ISI determined how to distribute these weapons among the mujahideen parties, and as such the ISI gave more weapons to the mujahideen forces they favored.[10] After the UN National Assembly met, the council overwhelmingly voted to call for an end to the armed invasion of Afghanistan by immediately withdrawing Soviet troops. However, President Brezhnev argued that the deployment of troops was not an invasion but rather was in accordance with Article 51 of the UN Charter, arguing that it was the right of the Afghan government and not of the United Nations to determine the status of the Soviet troops.[11]

As a result, the United States began providing covert assistance to the Afghan resistance fighters via Pakistan as early as January 1980. Furthermore, the American government supplied to Pakistan an emergency shipment of Stinger antiaircraft missiles for border protection against Soviet aerial assault and bombardment.[12] During this assistance, a wealthy Saudi businessman named Osama bin Laden was a central organizer and financial supporter of the mujahideen and provided the rebel forces with money, weapons, training, and additional fighters from around the world. Bin Laden's office, known as the Maktab al-Khadamat (MAK), provided these vital services and support for Afghanistan because of the fundamentalist Islamic penchant in Saudi Arabia. Bin Laden played a limited role in the Soviet resistance, and in 1988 he separated from the MAK to form al-Qaeda, with other militant members, with the intention of spearheading the anti-Soviet resistance into a global Islamic advancement.

As the primary champion for the mujahideen, Ahmed Shah Masood was a legendary military commander in Afghanistan who lived not only to fight the Soviets but also to fight against the Taliban. Under the fight waged by Masood, the mujahideen forces were heavily armed, well trained, and supported mainly by the United States and Pakistan. The leaders of the mujahideen devoted a great deal of training and operational efforts to sabotage warfare. These efforts included deliberate damage to power lines and pipelines and even included the bombing of government office buildings. The mujahideen groups focused on destroying the bridges and major roadways that the Soviets used and further attacked police stations and Soviet artillery posts. During the mid-1980s, the mujahideen forces increased their operational activities against the Soviets, and estimates over a two-year span from 1985 to 1987 reveal more than 1,800 episodes of mujahideen-initiated terrorist acts. The mujahideen also relied heavily on mine warfare, and with all these efforts to force the Soviets out of their country, the mujahideen often enlisted the aid of children and local villagers to assist in the attack Soviet military installations and air bases. As a result, the Soviets often mercilessly attacked all Afghan residents, blurring the line between the innocent Afghan citizens and the mujahideen rebels by performing blanket attacks on everyone.

While war may be considered a brutal necessity to life, the tactics the Soviets used throughout the invasion were often deemed as cruel to the point of being inhumane. One such measure was the use of "butterfly traps," which were tiny bomblike devices that were decorated and painted brightly to look like small toys. The Soviets designed these devices primarily with the intention of luring little children into picking them up. The traps were meant not to kill but rather to injure and maim so that the individual would require a great deal of care and attention. The rationale behind such contraptions was due to the amount of required medical care, funding, and time to assist an injured individual rather than the shorter amount of time needed to bury a dead body. The Soviets intentionally used these devices to harm children, believing that the most powerful fighter would abandon the call to defend Islam if his own child were injured.[13] For many foreign countries around the world, it was despicable that these traps were designed like toys to lure and maim innocent children. For the Soviets, however, the children were not innocent; rather, they were seen as a threat, for even young boys were trained with weapons and in combat techniques to support the mujahideen rebels. Even in this regard, the Soviets captured more than 40,000 Afghan youths and relocated them to the Soviet Union for the purpose of being raised as Soviets and being integrated into the "Soviet way of life."[14] Not only was it increasingly difficult for the Afghans to witness the capture of such young Afghan children, but the lacking medical facilities in Afghanistan contributed to the difficulty of helping those wounded by such heinous butterfly mine contraptions, and those scarce facilities that did exist were in deplorable condition. Even while trying to help the men and children who were wounded in battle, death was common from such minor ailments as heatstroke, hepatitis, and dysentery. Furthermore, the Soviets would invade towns and villages to annihilate mujahideen forces that may be residing in or near the town. Rather than guard the village against these freedom fighters, the Soviets would destroy the villages and kill all the inhabitants. If the mujahideen fighters escaped death from the Soviet raids in the villages, the Soviets would set up buried mines so that if the mujahideen did return, they would be killed or injured by the buried bombs waiting for them.

In May 1985, the seven main mujahideen rebel parties united and formed the Seven Party Mujahideen Alliance, also referred to as the Peshawar Seven. Eventually, the party became known as the Islamic Unity of Afghan Mujahideen, which sought to act as a diplomatic representation to the world. In the United Nations, the party sought representation as the Organization of Islamic Conference. The members of the Mujahideen Alliance were composed of two sects as either the political Islamics or the traditionalists.[15] The Mujahideen Alliance was active around Kabul, previously working to coordinate their anti-Soviet operations by administering rocket attacks against the government. Postwar estimates reveal that as many as 800 rockets were launched per day on communist government targets.

Throughout the nine years of occupation, the Soviets tried to hide their casualty and wounded numbers so that the Afghan forces would not know the severity of these attacks on the communist army. Early in the conflict, the Soviet forces faced major challenges in the mountainous terrain of Afghanistan. The Soviet army was unfamiliar with this type of mountainous combat, and as such the Soviet armored cars and tanks operated with extreme difficulty and were nearly impossible to maneuver. For the most part, the Soviet army was extremely ineffective and highly susceptible to attack in the mountains. In addition, the Soviets forced those who were injured to be secretly moved to undercover facilities in order to receive care covertly.

After Mikhail Gorbachev assumed the leadership of the Soviet Union early in 1985, the new leader looked for a way to withdraw gracefully from Afghanistan. With the increasing casualty toll, the severe loss of economic resources, and little Soviet support for the war, this graceful endeavor was nearly impossible for Gorbachev. As such, the Soviet Union looked to blame Babrak Karmal for his failure in instituting a communist regime in Afghanistan. The Soviets tried to shift the blame for their failure on Babrak's puppet regime by citing his ineffective rule and his inability to lead a destabilized Afghan government that was already weakened under the PDPA. In May 1986, Babrak was forced to resign as secretary-general of the PDPA, finally succumbing to the political pressures of the Soviet Union. His tenure as president would shortly end as well, given that in November 1986 the former chief of the Afghan secret police (known as KHAD) was elected as the fourth and last president of the communist-based DRA. Under the control of his communist advisers from the Soviet Union, President Mohammad Najibullah implemented a policy of "national reconciliation" between the Soviet forces and the rebelling Afghan people.

RETREAT OF SOVIET FORCES AND THE AFGHAN CIVIL WAR: 1988–1992

For more than 100 years, the Soviet government had tried to break apart Afghanistan and coerce the country into a communist state. By the end of the invasion in Afghanistan in 1987, Soviet aircraft were being destroyed on a regular basis, the Soviet army's casualties increased along with the cost of the war, and the Soviet people were calling for the need to abandon the conflict in Afghanistan. For these reasons, the futile Soviet invasion of Afghanistan is often referred to as the Soviet Union's Vietnam. Yet the Soviet government refused to withdraw forces from Afghanistan until 1988, with the final troops leaving on February 15, 1989. As the last of the Soviet forces left Afghanistan, more than 620,000 had served in the country over the nine-year occupation, with the total number of troops occupying Afghanistan at one time peaking at slightly more than 100,000. Throughout the war, more than 469,000 troops were wounded or fell ill, and the Soviet Union reported that 14,453 troops had been killed in Afghanistan and that between 10,700 and 11,600 were left disabled or as invalids after the war, numbers that are much smaller than those of U.S. soldiers lost in the Vietnam War. Contrastingly, the mujahideen reported losses of 1 million to 1.5 million, and tens of thousands were seriously wounded or crippled after the invasion.

The retreat of the Soviet army marked the beginning of Afghan Civil War from 1989 to 1992. Although they did remove their forces from Afghanistan, the Soviets continued to aid the Afghan government, which was now under the control of Mohammad Najibullah. The Afghan Civil War continued after the Soviet forces retreated during the harsh winter in Afghanistan, as the Afghan resistance still hungered to attack towns and cities to continue their war to defeat the Kabul government. As a result, President Najibullah declared a state of emergency in Afghanistan immediately after the Soviet withdrawal. Interestingly enough, the Soviet Union responded with a massive amount of military and economic supplies in addition to providing food and fuel for the subsequent two winters. By 1990, the amount of Soviet support provided after the war was approximately $3 billion after the Soviets had dispensed some $45 billion into Afghanistan during the nine-year struggle.[16] While never fully achieving popular support, Najibullah was able to defend the Afghan government from mujahideen attacks for three years from 1989 to 1992. Najibullah was finally defeated in 1992 when the newly reconstituted Russia refused to sell oil products to Afghanistan, thus blocking the much-needed food and fuel during the winter. The government in Kabul was now in a stalemate, and furthermore the defection of General Abdul Rashid Dostam to support Ahmed Shah Massoud gravely weakened Najibullah's government. The following month, the deteriorated government at Kabul finally succumbed to the mujahideen forces led by Dostam and Massoud, and Najibullah and his communist-funded government were overthrown. On April 18, 1992, the two men took control of Kabul and declared the Islamic State of Afghanistan. Sibghatullah Mojaddedi was named the interim leader of the Islamic State of Afghanistan after the fall of the communist regime in 1992. The Afghan rebel forces regarded his meeting with then U.S. President George H. W. Bush as a critical victory, and the solution for peace was a complete removal of the Kabul government. However, Mojaddedi served for only two months after transferring his presidential power to President Burhanuddin Rabbani for four years, a move that was based on a previous agreement of the mujahideen forces in Pakistan. The disorder and chaos that took place for the control of Kabul fostered the rise of the Taliban regime in Afghanistan.

NOTES

1. Norm Dixon, "How the CIA Created Osama Bin Laden," *Green Left Weekly,* September 19, 2001.

2. John Keegan, "The Ordeal of Afghanistan," *Atlantic Monthly,* November 1985.

3. Martin Ewans, *Afghanistan: A Short History of Its People and Politics.*

4. Robert D. Kaplan, *Soldiers of God: With Islamic Warriors in Afghanistan and Pakistan.*

5. Ewans, *Afghanistan.* As referenced in the author's notations, there are multiple variations of the Dubs incident, and the allegations range from the internal Afghan political parties to the plotting of the Soviet and U.S. intelligence communities.

6. Larry Goodson, *Afghanistan's Endless War: State Failure, Regional Politics, and the Rise of the Taliban.* By the spring of 1979, 24 of the 28 provinces in Afghanistan suffered outbreaks of tribal rebellion. See also Stephen Tanner, *Afghanistan: A Military History from Alexander the Great to the Fall of the Taliban.*

7. Keegan, "The Ordeal of Afghanistan." The author alleges that Amin killed Taraki by suffocating him with a pillow, while other accounts are not clear as to exactly what unfolded between Amin and Taraki over the course of the usurpation.

8. Ewans, *Afghanistan.* The author explains via the accounts of Raja Anwar, who was imprisoned in Pul-i-Charki with some of Amin's family members, which describe somewhat ambiguously the events on December 27 over the

killing of Hafizullah Amin. In his account, Amin and his family had fallen ill from a lunch banquet prepared by Soviet cooks. The Soviets did not intend to kill him but did give him the option to go into exile or to serve under Babrak Kamal. Amin either died from the refusal of these alternatives or had already been killed from unintentional poisoning. The author additionally argues that the Soviets would not have killed Amin if he had requested Soviet assistance, which is what alleged Afghan accounts have argued for killing their Islamic leader.

9. Goodson, *Afghanistan's Endless War*. The author discusses the continual landing of aircraft into Kabul Airport for Soviet troop deployment, and by early January more than 4,000 flights had landed in Kabul. In addition, by the beginning of 1980, more than 45,000 members of the Afghan army had deserted or joined the rebel forces.

10. Kaplan, *Soldiers of God*. Moreover, the ISI distributed weapons to the mujahideen commanders, whom they could easily control.

11. Steve Cool, *Ghost Wars: The Secret History of the CIA, Afghanistan, and bin Laden, from the Soviet Invasion to September 10, 2001*. The author argues against President Brezhnev's position and, as other critics have stated, against the hypocrisy of the Soviets' trying to legitimize the occupation since Amin would not champion for aid from the Soviets, only to be assassinated.

12. Keegan, "The Ordeal of Afghanistan." The Stinger is a short-range man-held missile known for its portability as an infrared surface-to-air homing device. The United States supplied these missiles to provide Pakistan with the ability to stop aerial skirmishes along the border with the Soviet Union and to prevent further bombing raids by the Soviets.

13. Kaplan, *Soldiers of God*. These butterfly mines are decorative and designed to attract children, and the author examines the statements of a Red Cross doctor who witnessed the heinous aftermath of these toylike mines.

14. Keegan, "The Ordeal of Afghanistan." The Soviets tried to relocate Afghan youths and force them into a communist upbringing. The Soviets perhaps intended to return these youths to Afghanistan one day after they had been conditioned to Soviet rule in order to assist the Soviets in controlling and subduing the native Afghan people.

15. Kaplan, *Soldiers of God*. These political parties were not respected by some Afghan citizens, arguing that the war for Afghan independence should be fought on the battlefield and not as an armchair warrior in a conference room. The political Islamics were divided into four fundamentalist groups: the Islamic Party led by Yunus Khalis, the Islamic Party led by Gulbuddin Hekmatyar, the Islamic Society led by Burhanuddin Rabbani, and the Islamic Union for the Liberation of Afghanistan led by Rasul Sayyaf.

16. Ahmed Rashid, *Taliban: Militant Islam, Oil, and Fundamentalism in Central Asia*.

such, despite their withdrawal, the Soviets continued to support President Najibullah of Afghanistan until the mujahideen forces led by Rashid Dostam and Ahmed Shah Massoud gained control of Kabul. The capture of the capital was a devastating blow to the Pashtuns, who had held control of the city for nearly 300 years.[1] For the next two years until the rise of the Taliban, Afghanistan descended into chaos.

Throughout the Soviet conflict, many of Afghanistan's elite and intellectual members of society fled the country as refugees and sought exile in the neighboring countries of Pakistan and, to a less significant degree, in Iran. After the collapse of the Najibullah government, refugees sought to return to the country, and the numbers are particularly staggering for the six-month period after the overthrow of Najibullah. The return began in April 1992, with the rush of refugees returning from Pakistan totaling 1.2 million throughout the spring and the summer. With the influx of people came the overarching sentiment of lawlessness, massive poverty, and the destruction of cities, particularly in Kabul. Women were most susceptible to attack and rape, which occurred even in broad daylight. Many young Afghan girls who were barely 16 had been repeatedly kidnapped and raped by the mujahideen forces, often being taken in the night and then stripped, raped, and beaten by gangs of mujahideen.[2] Women were afraid to report these rapes and beatings, fearing further punishment or even death. Resistance to these mujahideen rebels was forthcoming, and by 1994 more than 10,000 people had been killed in Kabul alone.

In 1994, the friction among the leaders of the multiple mujahideen factions resulted in a period of warlordism in Afghanistan. As these leaders fought for power among themselves to control the roadways between Pakistan and Afghanistan, they captured much-needed food and relief shipments and sold these supplies on the black market. Further, mujahideen rebels set up checkpoints along the roadways and levied tolls that travelers had to pay. Sometimes these checkpoints were only a few miles apart because of multiple mujahideen forces each trying to receive the most amount of money, and if these travelers did not have enough currency to make it through all the checkpoints, they were beaten and sometimes killed. The chaos in the country gave rise to the Taliban, which means "student" or the more glamorized "seekers of knowledge." The Taliban was originally formed as a Sunni Muslim puritanical movement composed of Pashtun students from the southern Helmand and Kandahar regions in Afghanistan. The primary goal of the Taliban was to impose a strict allegiance to Islamic law, and as such they developed a politico-religious force, and almost 98 percent were of the Pashtuns of southern Afghanistan and also from northwestern Pakistan. The Taliban received training in weaponry and combat from the Pakistani government under Pakistan's Inter-Services Intelligence. By 1996, the Taliban seized control in Kabul under the Islamic Emirate of Afghanistan. Four years later, the Taliban had successfully extended their control throughout 95 percent of the country until being toppled by the Northern Alliance fighters and American aerial bombardment.

THE ORIGIN OF THE SEEKERS OF KNOWLEDGE: 1994–1996

Many westerners might be surprised that the Taliban originally formed with the noble intention to unify the country under a purity stance toward Islamic rule. Since the retreat of the Soviets, many Afghans had grown tired of the corruption, fighting, and brutality of the mujahideen warlords and the toleration for such acts by a country that had little choice in the matter. Before the official formation of the Taliban, a Muslim cleric named Mohammad Omar was revolted at the disturbing news of several mujahideen men who had captured two young girls and were holding them hostage and subjecting the young girls to rape and torture. Angered by the five years of corruption and debauchery that these so-called Islamic warriors had brought to Afghanistan, Omar gathered about 50 students from local *madrassas* (regarded as religious schools or seminaries) and led these young students into the mujahideen camp, freeing the teenage girls and hanging two of the mujahideen offenders. Two months later, Omar led these students again into Kandahar to rescue a young boy suffering the same fate by the intolerable mujahideen. Revitalized by creating this wave of defeat against the southern mujahideen forces in Afghanistan, the Taliban officially banded together and set out to conquer the remaining cities around the country and end the corruption. For many, the newly formed Taliban was a wave of hope that these students would unite the country in peace and put an end to the insufferable acts endured under the mujahideen warlords. The first true act of the Taliban occurred in October 1994 when the Pakistani government sent an armored convoy to Turkmenistan via Herat and Kandahar. Armed mujahideen warlords attacked the convoy, but the Taliban ambushed the mujahideen aggressors, overcame these forces, and allowed the convoy to continue into Kandahar. The Taliban proceeded into the city as well, fighting the mujahideen forces and overcoming them by killing many of the leaders and imprisoning the others. The Taliban announced the movement in Kandahar to free the country from the overarching corruption that had plagued this land and further sought to bring the Islamic way of life to Afghanistan.

After the mujahideen warlords surrendered, the Taliban worked quickly to issue policies that would bring Afghanistan back to an Islamic-centered way of life. For men, these requirements included wearing turbans and no longer shaving their beards. Women were required to wear the burqa at all times in public, and if they were to go outside the home (which was not encouraged), they had to be accompanied by a male blood relative. Women were not allowed to work since their sole purpose was to raise the future Muslims of Afghanistan. Since the employment of women was outlawed and women were the primary teachers in Afghanistan, many schools for both girls and boys were closed. However, these schools eventually opened again and operated in secrecy.[3] In 1995, Omar announced that the Taliban would be more than just a political force against the mujahideen. He desired the Taliban to act as warriors in a jihad against the Muslims and non-Muslims who harmed the Afghan people. As the leader of the Taliban, he vowed to lead these forces across the country to implement Islamic order. The Taliban repeated this method throughout the cities of Afghanistan, and their reputation for allowing bloodless retreat enabled these religious zealots to overcome mujahideen forces with relatively little effort. The Taliban was also assisted by instructing a smaller force to march ahead to the village and announce the impending arrival of the Taliban. Thus, they encountered little resistance, and furthermore most villagers were glad to assist the Taliban in eliminating the extortionate comrades of the mujahideen, as these weary Afghans had not experienced any form of peace since 1979. Thousands of supporters flocked to join the Taliban, strongly optimistic at the sight of the mujahideen forces that gave up and vanished into the mountains of Afghanistan. Further, Taliban support increased from the students of madrassas in Pakistan who crossed the border to join their Afghan brethren. The turning point for the Taliban occurred when Omar and his supporters finally mustered enough strength to capture the capital of Kabul in September 1996.

THE SPREAD OF THE TALIBAN AND THE WAR WITH THE NORTHERN ALLIANCE: 1996–2001

The era from 1996 to 2001 under the control of the Taliban may be regarded as one of the darkest periods in the history of Afghanistan. During this time, only three countries offered diplomatic recognition: the United Arab Emirates, Pakistan, and Saudi Arabia. The majority of the other surrounding countries opposed the Taliban and associated with the Northern Alliance, and these countries included Iran, India, Turkey, Russia, and Central Asia. The Taliban swept across Afghanistan, removing mujahideen in city after city in a dominating yet bloodless manner. As support increased substantially, the Afghan people championed and welcome these Islamic students for finally eliminating the plague of Islamic warriors in Afghanistan without much violence. It was therefore a severe shock and surprising upset to the community when the Taliban stormed into Kabul and violently demonstrated how the Taliban would punish enemies and offenders of the Islamic faith. The death of Mohammad Najibullah was a symbolic gesture for the Taliban and serves as the first demonstration of the horrific power the Taliban possessed as they infiltrated the streets of Afghanistan. The Taliban used Najibullah as an example. They publicly beat him, tied his feet to a Jeep, and then dragged him through the rocky and jagged streets. The next morning, Afghan residents were shocked to witness the dead, bloated body hanging from a traffic light, his neck so swollen from the beatings and the Afghan sun that the steel noose continued to cut into his flesh. While many citizens were surprised at such a ghastly execution, Najibullah was an abhorred figure in the politics of Afghanistan, and as such the Taliban was still viewed positively.

While the Taliban overpowered southern Afghanistan with few episodes of violence, the regime changed after moving into the north after seizing control in Kabul. The Taliban worked to defeat anchor cities such as Mazari Sharif, and in this instance they did not send advance forces to offer bloodless collaboration with the Taliban. Instead, they sent their message by firing rockets and missiles into the city. In 1997, the legendary mujahideen leader Ahmad Shah Massoud developed a plan to infiltrate and destroy the Taliban regime north of Kabul in the Shamali plains. Massoud infiltrated the villagers who once pledged allegiance to the Taliban, and in doing so he turned these peaceful dwellings into camouflaged ensnarements. As a result, the Taliban forces arrived in the Shamali plains and walked into a surprising ambush by the villagers and Massoud's forces. However, nearly a year later in August 1998, the Taliban returned to defeat these forces in the city. Known as the massacre of Mazari Sharif, the Taliban sought vengeance on their previous downfall by ruthlessly slaughtering thousands of Afghan citizens and several Iranian diplomats, and the episode is regarded as the worst civilian abomination in the history of the country. Several months before the massacre, the Taliban controlled nearly 75 percent of Afghanistan, and, more important, they controlled the major roadways into Pakistan.[4] The Taliban proudly declared that the pagans had been slaughtered for their treason against Islam, and after the massacre of Mazari Sharif, the Northern Alliance held only a small amount of land in Afghanistan with approximately 90 percent being in control of the Taliban.

The majority of the population lost all forms of independence in addition to many forms of human rights, and as such the Taliban moved from a hub of optimism to a center of controversy over these policies. Omar enforced his rule through the Ministry of the Promotion of Virtue and the Prevention of Vice (PVPV). The Taliban was notorious in their treatment and policies toward women, and as such women lost any form of freedom, including the ability to work and receive an education after the age of eight. The Taliban's interpretation of Muslim law enforced the *hejab*, which required women to be secluded from society, and if they were to be in public, women must be covered by a garment that respected Islamic law more than the *chador*, which exposed the facial area. Under the Taliban's interpretation of the *Sharia* (Islamic law), women were forced to wear the Afghan burqa at all times in public, designed by the Taliban's interpretation and enforcement of Islamic law. The burqa is a head-to-toe garment that must cover every inch of a woman's skin and is different than the Pakistan or Iranian form of the burqa, in which the face and eyes are exposed. The rule of the Taliban was so extreme that while a woman was walking on the road one day, she exposed her hand briefly enough to reveal the nail polish on her fingertips. As punishment for her violation against the code of the Taliban and insult against Islam, several Taliban men held her down and cut off the tips of her fingers. Furthermore, those who resisted the Taliban rule were severely punished, as was the case when a group of women protested the Taliban in Herat. As these women marched through the streets protesting the Islamic law of the Sharia, Taliban members surrounded the leader, doused her with kerosene, and set her on fire to serve as a symbol for what would happen to women if they disobeyed. Women who were caught wearing nail polish, makeup, or even white socks under their burqas were punished by being covered in acid or beaten with cutting wire.[5] For other crimes, such as stealing even minor items, these offenders almost immediately had their hands or feet cut off, depending on the severity of the crime or, in some cases, the monetary value of the stolen items. These amputations were held in public locations where the offender was given a minor numbing agent while their limbs were severed from their bodies and then proudly displayed to the crowd. In some cases, attempts were made at nearby hospitals to reattach these limbs, but overwhelmingly these attempts were not successful.

However, women injured in such punishments sometimes were not able to receive medical treatment, even in the dismal medical facilities that existed in Afghanistan, since male doctors were banned from treating women unless they were accompanied by a male chaperone. In many cases, women were turned away for medical care for this reason alone. Furthermore, hospital wards were segregated for women, as they could not be near male patients, and often the female wards were located in a dimly lit basement. Regardless of the medical situation, gender was always the dominant medical infirmity during the rule of the Taliban.[6] Female doctors had long been chased out of the hospitals, and the painfully lacking medical facilities for women and were severely limited and often unable to help women in childbirth. Not surprisingly, many women died from infections due to the inhumane and unsanitary conditions, which included buildings without running water and barely enough electricity to turn on the lights. The Taliban eventually allowed some female doctors to work, but even then the doctors were required to wear the burqa during operations and medical procedures. For the most part, these female doctors needed to remove these garments and would do so as long as they would not get caught. However, the PVPV squads savored the opportunity to catch female doctors who were not wearing burqas. Furthermore, because of overcrowding in some hospitals, the PVPV would order the women to leave the hospital first, even if it was a woman near death rather than a man with only minor injuries. The reasoning behind these feminine expulsions was that in these overcrowded conditions, the PVPV could not guarantee that these women could be protected amidst so many men. While many male doctors and dentists disagreed with the Taliban policies toward the medical treatment of women, many of these doctors were afraid to treat patients in the presence of the PVPV squad for fear of execution. Further, doctors were afraid of being reported, and as such women received little to no medical care.

In spite of the publicized atrocities that women endured throughout these years in Afghanistan, this does not imply that men escaped brutality under the Taliban regime. Men were ordered to grow full beards and were given only six weeks to do so after the Taliban announced this decree. Further, men were to be properly attired in public, which included the wearing of the *shalwars*, which are baggy trousers that must be a specific length just about the ankle. Furthermore, a man's beard could not be longer than his fist, and if his hair was too long, the PVPV stood on street corners with scissors and were prepared to cut the hair so that these men no longer offended Islam. Furthermore, the Taliban also ostracized any form of homosexuality, which was part of the reasoning behind Mohammad Omar's forming the Taliban due to the mujahideen notorious rape of young boys. The punishments included tying the offenders to a truck and parading them through the streets while their faces were blackened with engine oil, while the traditional method of punishment was to bring down a wall on the wrongdoers.[7] While these reprimands might be viewed as perplexing to a Western observer, the punishments for these homosexual acts were fundamental for Islamists and based on the Taliban's understanding of Islamic law.

THE RISE OF THE DRUG TRADE IN AFGHANISTAN

During the period of Afghan civil war, the country was severely starving and relied on food supplies sent from Pakistan and other world relief organizations. However, the mujahideen forces frequently captured these shipments and sold these goods on the black market, charging outrageous sums for food that should have been freely administered to the Afghan population. Furthermore, in the mujahideen's quest to acquire more money, the warlords forced the Afghan farmers to cease growing crops and food products and ordered them to cultivate poppies, desiring the higher income achieved from the drug production rather than from the crop harvest. The mujahideen did not care that the majority of Afghanistan was starving as long as the profits from the drug trade were increasing. Resilient and brave farmers who continued to grow crops and to plant orchards were killed and their homes razed to the ground. Those farmers who did comply received very little of the opium prof-its and were still left in poverty. Under the reign of the mujahideen warlords, drug production in Afghanistan skyrocketed to launch the country as the world's leading source of heroin and opium production, producing as much as 70 percent of the world's supply.

The Taliban's strict regime on religion, women, and education seem to be in complete contrast to the statements regarding their tolerance of drug produc-tion in Afghanistan. When the Taliban first assumed power in Kandahar, they quickly announced that the drug trade in Afghanistan must be eliminated. However, the Taliban soon realized that drug cultivation and production was imperative in order to pump much-needed income back into the economy and, more important, to fund their efforts. As such, accounts from multiple sources differ as to whether the Taliban encouraged or prohibited the cultiva-tion of opium poppies in Afghanistan. When the Taliban set out to end the corruption of the mujahideen, estimates reveal that the Taliban controlled 96 percent of the poppy cultivation in Afghanistan and further reaped substantial profits by taxing the farmers. In addition, poppy refiners produced morphine and heroin to transport to the West, and the Taliban further taxed and levied fees on the transport of these goods.[8] The result of these taxes created tens of millions of dollars in revenue for the Taliban per year. Other accounts allege that Taliban officials punished anyone involved in the production and smug-gling of hashish since these users were mainly Muslim. However, according to Abdul Rashid, the chief of the Taliban's antidrug force in Kandahar, the Taliban allowed farmers to grow opium to produce heroin since these drugs were consumed by the *kafirs* (infidels) in the West and not by the Afghan Muslims.[9] Thus, under Islamic law, the Taliban justified that they were free to continue poppy cultivation only for the sale of opium, and thus the Taliban could continue to collect the large sums of money this generated since opium was not used by Muslims.

OSAMA BIN LADEN AND THE AFGHAN CAMPS

While the Taliban may have started under good intentions, the arrival of Osama bin Laden in Afghanistan in 1996 would drastically impact the future of the Taliban. When the Taliban finally gained momentum in the siege of Kabul of 1996, bin Laden sought to form an alliance with these Islamic funda-mentalists and his al-Qaeda organization, and he continued to build terrorist camps free from the government oversight that he had to endure in Saudi Arabia. The Taliban was equally fundamentalist and shared the same views with bin Laden to defeat the infidels of the West. The Taliban welcomed bin Laden, and their support in terrorist acts resulted in the payment of millions of dollars from bin Laden. After establishing his home in southern Afghanistan, bin Laden raised the call to jihad against Saudi Arabia and the United States, stating that it was the duty of the Muslims to kill the American people and their allies.

The fact that bin Laden was willing to stand up to the United States was a beacon of hope for disillusioned young Afghan men. As such, from 1997 to 2001, the private army of the al-Qaeda guerrilla organization known as the 055 Brigade was integrated into the Taliban army and created multiple Afghan camps, most of which served as terrorist training camps to support the jihad. The camps were taught at multiple levels of education, and soldiers advanced at the discretion of their instructors and their evaluation of the student's skill and religious fervor. The Taliban and al-Qaeda toiled together to make a strong group of terrorists, and relations were further solidified when one of bin Laden's daughters married one of Mohammad Omar's sons, thus forming a representational allegiance in a matrimonial agreement.

These Afghan camps instructed students on covert terrorist operations in order to blend into the Western world of the infidels. Completely contradictory to their social upbringing, terrorist trainees were instructed on Western etiquette, such as being clean-shaven, taking showers, and wearing cologne to hide body odor to smell more appealing to westerners. Further, they were instructed to speak in code in case phone lines were tapped, using words such as "Canada" instead of "Afghanistan" or using "playing with balloons" to refer to terrorist-related activities as part of the jihad. Bin Laden continued to finance and support the Taliban regime, and he is believed to have been the mastermind behind several terrorist activities around the world. These offenses include the 1998 American Embassy bombings in Dar es Salaam, Tanzania, and the bombing in Nairobi, Kenya. After these bombings, bin Laden and several members of al-Qaeda were indicted in a U.S. criminal court, but the Taliban protected bin Laden from the extradition requests, making ambiguous statements that he had gone missing and even arguing that there was no proof in the allegations and indictment of these terrorist activities. Furthermore, the bombing of the USS *Cole* while it was docked in Yemen was not officially accredited to al-Qaeda, but bin Laden publicly praised the attack.

THE DEATH OF THE LION OF PANJSHIR AND THE COLLAPSE OF THE TALIBAN

Ahmad Shah Massoud and his Northern Alliance forces are what prevented the Taliban from controlling the entire country of Afghanistan. Massoud was by far the most esteemed fighter of the Northern Alliance, earning him the respectful title of "The Lion of Panjshir." Not only was Massoud a brilliant strategist against the Soviets and the Taliban, but he genuinely cared for the safety of his fighters. As such, he ordered his commanders to allow only men who were not married, who had no children, or who were not the only sons in the family to be selected for dangerous missions against the Taliban. On September 9, 2001, the revered Northern Alliance military leader was killed when two suicide bombers and believed supporters of al-Qaeda posed as interviewers and blew themselves up in front of Massoud.

The Taliban was implicated as terrorists, and as part of their terrorist regime, the group was condemned for the continual harboring of bin Laden and his al-Qaeda network. After the September 11 attacks on the World Trade Center in New York and the Pentagon in Washington, D.C., the United States quickly implemented its response under the military campaign Operation Enduring Freedom. As part of this objective and in uniting with the Northern Alliance, the United States sought to eliminate the Taliban regime and al-Qaeda in Afghanistan. By November 2001, the Taliban had been removed from power in the country. Although bin Laden has not been captured and presumably is seeking refuge in the mountains of Afghanistan, the Taliban was driven from its last seat of power in Kandahar and forced to retreat to the wilderness of Afghanistan as a guerilla warfare operation. Currently, these Taliban forces continue to recruit new forces and work to devise plans to restore their power in Afghanistan.

The following month, plans were outlined to institute a new democratic government in Afghanistan, and in the interim, the future President Hamid Karzai was established as the chairman of the Afghan Interim Authority. Furthermore, in a loya jirga in 2002, Karzai was chosen as the interim president of Afghanistan until the new elections would be held after the establishment and ratification of a new constitution for the country. However, as testament to the resentment still lingering in the shadows, Vice President Haji Abdul Qadir was assassinated in July 2002 outside his government office.

DEMOCRATIC ELECTIONS: 2004

For many Afghan citizens, the dawn of a promising era began when the country held the first historically significant national democratic elections in October 2004. The determination of the national assembly allowed Afghanistan to become an Islamic republic, but after centuries of mayhem, many Afghans are still distrustful of any type of political control. Several ethnic groups hold their own opinion on how Afghanistan should be governed, including the Pashtuns, the Tajiks, and the Hazaras. As history has proven, when these groups are not consulted in political situations or are consulted and ignored, these ethnic tribes do not hesitate to respond in the form of rebellion.

This new democratically elected government seeks to unite and reconstruct Afghanistan while simultaneously eliminating the turmoil and harbored violence within the country. In spite of the many obstacles the country faces in rebuilding, even with the Taliban no longer in control but still a threat, hope remains on the horizon. Many citizens viewed the 2002 loya jirga and the democratic election in 2004, which officially elected Karzai as president, as further propelling the country into a better and more promising future.

NOTES

1. Ahmed Rashid, *Taliban: Militant Islam, Oil, and Fundamentalism in Central Asia.*

2. Sally Armstrong, *Veiled Threat: The Hidden Power of the Women of Afghanistan.*

3. Peter Marsden, *The Taliban: War, Religion and the New Order in Afghanistan.* Men were also forced into certain dress protocols and were also required to pray five times a day to Mecca in order to receive a higher degree of Islamic observance. The Religious Police banned "not praying at prayer times," and if caught, the offender was severely punished for insulting Islamic law.

4. Neamatollah Nojumi, *The Rise of the Taliban in Afghanistan: Mass Mobilization, Civil War, and the Future of the Region.* The massacre is widely believed to have been a form of ethnic cleansing against the Hazara people, as the Taliban was adamantly opposed to these descendants of the Mongols and especially targeted this ethnicity.

5. Armstrong, *Veiled Threat.* For the women who were caught wearing nail polish under the burqa, they were considered lucky if they received only a public beating by the Taliban. The typical white socks under the burqa could not be worn since the Taliban's flag was white and therefore a holy color that represented the purity of the regime.

6. Cheryl Bernard, *Veiled Courage: Inside the Afghan Women's Resistance.* Women in the hospital who gave birth to female babies were often punished by being seemingly abandoned in the hospital by their husbands, often left alone at the hospital for a week. The logic behind this tactic is that for her next pregnancy, the woman will want to make sure she delivers a boy to the family and will not dishonor them by giving birth to a girl again. As students of biology know, the father supplies the Y chromosome, which is the chromosome needed to produce a male child.

7. Rashid, *Taliban.* The Hazaras especially suffered under the beard requirement since their biological and chemical makeup did not foster the growth of a full beard. As such, they were frequently targeted and punished for this offense against Islam.

10

Democracy and the Future of Afghanistan

Years of war, devastation, and conflict have saturated the history of Afghanistan. During the 19th century, the confrontation between the expanding British and Russian empires for territory in Central Asia drastically impacted the history, culture, and environment of Afghanistan. While the country was used mainly as a pawn in the Great Game, Afghanistan often served as a buffer state in the midst of the surrounding Anglo-Afghan aggression and the lack of concern for the Afghan people. The 20th century continued the tension and warfare with the Third Anglo-Afghan Civil War in 1919, the result of which at least solidified Afghanistan's independence from the British and heralded respect from neighboring countries. The Soviets, however, continued their struggle for control of the country, finally cumulating in the Soviet invasion in 1979. For 10 years, the country endured a communist-controlled government, savage war techniques, and constant bombardment and destruction. Finally, the mujahideen forces successfully worked to cast out the Soviets, but the retreat of the Soviet forces was just the beginning of the mayhem to come. The Afghan Civil War from 1989 to 1992 was a time of corruption, rape, and disillusionment as the mujahideen forces turned on each other to gain control of the country. The constant corruption and bribery the mujahideen required was bitterly hated among the Afghan citizens who were caught in the middle. When the Taliban regime surfaced to expel these corrupt warlords, the country welcomed these religious madrassa students with open arms. However, once the Taliban united with the fundamentalists of al-Qaeda, Afghanistan was thrust into an Islamic maelstrom of darkness and despair.

PROBLEMS FOR THE COUNTRY IN THE 21ST CENTURY

The United States seemingly obliterated the Taliban forces in December 2001 to open the gates for a new assembly in Afghanistan. The country once again emerged into the international community, and as such, the leaders worked to establish diplomatic relations with countries that could not support Afghanistan under the fundamentalist Islamic State of Afghanistan as created by the Taliban. One year after overthrowing the Taliban regime and forcing the militants into exile, Afghanistan signed the Kabul Declaration on Good Neighborly Relations with the nearby countries of Iran, Pakistan, China, Turkmenistan, Uzbekistan, and Tajikistan. The declaration was a symbolic agreement that respected and upheld Afghanistan's independence and territorial boundaries. Furthermore, countries all around the world, including the United States and Japan, have pledged financial support to assist in the rebuilding of the devastated land in which fields, orchards, and villages have been destroyed. The rebuilding efforts are underway, but in many areas these efforts are not occurring quickly enough, and many estimates state that it may take up to 10 years to completely rebuild Afghanistan. As it stands currently, the country continues to be one of the poorest and least developed countries in the world.

However, as the government continues plans to rebuild and restore Afghanistan, the country struggles against such impediments as poverty, poor economic infrastructure, land mines, and a huge illegal opium production and trade. The country continues to grapple with the Taliban insurgency scheming in the shadows while devising new plans to overthrow the government and control Afghanistan once more. Further, attacks are a frequent occurrence from the few remaining al-Qaeda and Taliban militants, and insurgents continue to plan such devastating tactics as suicide bombings. Health issues continue to plague the nation, and while medical facilities have substantially improved, these efforts are not enough. Because the Taliban regime, for more than five years, required women to stay inside, many women are unhealthy and require substantial medical treatment. Having been covered from head to toe in the burqa, some women in Afghanistan suffer from osteomalacia, a softening of the bones due to an insufficient diet and a lack of sunlight.

The Taliban still lingers on the horizon, waiting for the opportunity to come back and crush the U.S.-supported Afghan government. In early 2007, the Taliban's increasing presence in Afghanistan led the U.S. government to consider longer military tours of duty and even increasing the number of troops deployed in the country. However, the problems of Afghanistan can not be resolved only by increasing the military presence and support. The number of insurgent attacks has steadily begun to increase, along with the illegal production of opium. In a surprising maneuver, President Karzai held negotiations with the Taliban in April 2007 amidst the long-standing dispute on how to rectify the situation with the Taliban. The main options have been to eradicate the regime through capture and execution or to work at peace negotiations and end the need to resolve conflicts with violence. As such, President Karzai sought approval from the U.S. and the North Atlantic Treaty Organization (NATO) before meeting with the Taliban leaders. However, many believe these peace talks should have occurred much earlier to foster more amicable relations and hinder attacks that occurred from the hands of the Taliban. As such, a gap has formed between the Tajiks of the north and the Taliban-inclined Pashtuns of the south.[1] The Taliban has increasingly grown stronger despite being officially removed by the Northern Alliance and U.S. forces. Furthermore, the allowance of neighboring countries to harbor pro-Taliban and al-Qaeda militants permits the Taliban to increase in strength and thus gain a stronger hold in the country.

Early in 2007, the Afghan government embarked on a quest to destroy the opium croplands in the country with a poppy eradication team. Already unpopular, the Karzai administration faces severe criticism for removing this generous source of income from the farmers without providing a realistic substitute income. The drug trade in Afghanistan has been lucrative, with figures in 2006 reaching an all-time high at more than 6,000 tons harvested. The previous all-time high occurred in 2005. As a result of these steadily increasing numbers, the government seeks to eliminate this illegal drug trade once and for all. This movement arrives after a survey of winter planting trends in Afghanistan indicated that 2007 could be the biggest crop yield to date. These estimates revealed an increase in half the agricultural provinces that planned to harvest more poppies in 2007.[2] In order to eliminate another bumper-crop year, the Karzai administration is diligently working to destroy these poppy fields.

Further significant obstacles for Afghanistan include the warlords who claim certain territories as their own. These warlords enslave the inhabitants of that region and for the most part operate beyond the control of the government. Removing the Taliban from power gave the warlords the opportunity to quickly claim these abandoned territories. These warlords, however, are split between enemies of the Taliban and silent supporters; however, regardless of which side they are found on, warlords are a severe threat to the new Afghan government and the stability of Afghanistan's future. In order to remove these warlords, who substantially contribute to the increasing illegal

Notable Figures in Afghanistan

Abdali, Ahmad Shah (1720–1772). First emir and ruler of Afghanistan from 1747 to 1772 and is considered to be the founder of modern Afghanistan. During his reign, he continuously worked to expand Afghanistan's borders and created an extensive empire that extended from eastern Persia to northern India. Elected as Ahmad Khan and assumed the name Ahmad Shah Durrani.

Alexander the Great (356 B.C.E.–323 B.C.E.). Considered one of the greatest military leaders in all of history, Alexander conquered most of the known world before his death. In 331 B.C.E., Alexander and his Greek armies deposed the Persian Empire and seized the land known today as Afghanistan.

Asoka the Great (304 B.C.E.–232 B.C.E.). Indian emperor and ruler of the Mauryan dynasty from 273 B.C.E. to 232 B.C.E. In 262 B.C.E. at the Battle of Kalinga, after witnessing great destruction and death, he abandoned the life of the sword and embraced Buddhism. His teachings and beliefs in moral behavior were widespread in the southern region of Afghanistan, and his teachings are carved on the Rock Pillar Edicts in such locations as Kandahar.

Bin Laden, Osama (1957–). Islamic militant and leader of al-Qaeda and is believed to be the mastermind behind the 9/11 attacks. Bin Laden and al-Qaeda have allegedly carried out a number of terrorist and guerrilla attacks worldwide, including the 9/11 attacks on the World Trade Center and the

Pentagon. Bin Laden is wanted by the FBI for his involvement in these attacks as well as for the 1998 U.S. Embassy bombings in Dar es Salaam, Tanzania, and Nairobi, Kenya, and also for other attacks around the world. His current whereabouts are unknown, but he is supposedly hiding in Afghanistan.

Cyrus the Great (590 B.C.E.–530 B.C.E.). Also known as Cyrus II of Persia, he is the founder of the Persian Empire. After conquering the Medes and assuming control of their lands, including in Afghanistan, Cyrus became king of Persia in 559 B.C.E.

Daoud, Zohra Yousuf (1954–). Former Afghani model who won the title of Miss Afghanistan and used her title to promote literacy throughout the country. She currently works as a social activist for women's rights in Afghanistan.

Darius III (380 B.C.E.–330 B.C.E.). Last king of the Archamenid Empire of Persia and rival of Alexander the Great. Sparring for many years with Alexander, Darius led the Persian army in the Battle of Gaugamela in 330 B.C.E. At the battle, Alexander the Great defeated the Persian Empire. Darius was chased off the battlefield by Alexander and ultimately defeated, but Darius was overthrown and killed by his trusted adviser Bessus.

Durand, Sir Henry Mortimer (1850–1924). Diplomat and civil servant to colonial British India and served as a political secretary in Kabul during the Second Anglo-Afghan War from 1878 to 1880. His is most notably remembered for his negations in 1893 with Amir Abdur Rahman of Afghanistan over what would come to be known as the Pashtunian issue. His self-created Durand line was an ethnographic delineation that separated the frontier province between British India and Afghanistan and eventually resulted in the international border between Afghanistan and Pakistan.

Hekmatyar, Gulbuddin (1947–). An Afghan warlord under the mujahideen forces and served as the prime minister twice during the 1990s. He was also the founder of the Hezb-i-Islami Party in 1975, and he is regarded for his measures against Soviet occupation as well as the United States. In 2003, the United States declared that Hekmatyar was a global terrorist and ally of Osama bin Laden.

Hotak, Mirwais Khan (1673–1715). A legendary figure and Afghan hero, he was the leader of the Ghilzai tribe and also mayor of Kandahar. In 1709, he assassinated Gurgin Khan, the Georgian governor and tyrant from the Persian court. After the assassination, Mirwais Khan successfully defeated the Persians and ejected them from Afghanistan. Mirwais remained in power until his death in 1715 and is regarded as Afghanistan's first nationalist. As a symbol of his historical significance in Afghanistan, he is entombed in a blue-domed mausoleum at Bagh-i-Kohkran outside Kandahar.

Kaniska I (304 B.C.E.–232 B.C.E.). Indian emperor and ruler of the Kushan dynasty from 273 B.C.E. to 232 B.C.E. He encouraged Asoka's beliefs in Buddhism and promoted a moral way of life. As tribute to Asoka's teachings and beliefs of Buddhism, King Kaniska had carved into the mountains two large Buddha's statues. Known as the "Buddhas at Bamyan," these gorgeous figures sadly were destroyed as part of the Taliban's regime in 2001.

Karmal, Babrak (1929–1996). He was the third president of Afghanistan from 1979 to 1986, reigning during the Soviet invasion of Afghanistan. Before his career in politics, he was arrested for his involvement in Marxist activities at Kabul University, and after his time in prison he became a devout communist and friend to the Soviets. Karmal was the leader of the communist regime Parcham after the split in the People's Democratic Party of Afghanistan in 1967.

Karzai, Hamid (1957–). Both the current and first democratically elected president of Afghanistan. After winning the election in December 2004, Karzai removed many of the former Northern Alliance warlords from his cabinet. He has been working to form a peace alliance with these warlords rather than fighting so that Afghanistan is not caught in another civil war.

Khalis, Younas Mohammad (1919–2006). As a devout fundamentalist, he assisted in the launching of the Taliban regime in Afghanistan as a mujahideen commander during the Soviet invasion of Afghanistan in 1979. Leader of the Hezb-i-Islami (the Party of Islam), which was the same as Gulbuddin Hekmatyar's party.

Khan, Abdur Rahman (1844–1901). Amir of Afghanistan from 1881 to 1901, he was a strong ruler who reestablished the Afghan government structure after the Second Anglo-Afghan War.

Khan, Amir Amanullah (1892–1960). Ruler of Afghanistan from 1919 to 1929 until he was overthrown by tribal forces and forced into exile. He is well known for leading Afghanistan in achieving complete independence from the British.

Khan, Daoud Mohammad (1793–1863). The first president of Afghanistan from 1973 to 1978 until being killed in a military coup by the Khalq regime. Previously served as the prime minister under King Zahir Shah until being forced to resign in 1963 because of his incessant involvement in the Pashtunian issue, which contributed to the failing economy in Afghanistan.

Khan, Dost Mohammad (1793–1863). He was regarded as an eminent player in the development of Central Asia, particularly as the founder of the Barakzai dynasty in Afghanistan, and ousted Mahmud Khan in 1826. Ruling during the First Anglo-Afghan War in Afghanistan, he was ousted from power by the British and forced into exile. After his surrender and subsequent release by the British, he formed a strong alliance with the Sikhs of India. He furthered Afghanistan's tribal efforts but died suddenly several months after his victory in Herat.

Khan, Genghis (ca. 1162–1227). Considered one of the most successful military leaders in all of history, he founded the largest contiguous empire, known as the Mongol Empire. The empire existed from 1206 to 1368, and Genghis invaded and ravaged the region of Afghanistan in 1219.

Lang, Timur (1336–1405). A fourteenth-century Mongol warrior and conqueror of much of western and Central Asia. Founder of the Timurid Empire in Central Asia, he conquered and dominated much of Afghanistan in the late fourteenth century. Because of an injury to his right leg, he was forced to limp, earning him the name Timur Lang, or Timur the Lame.

Massoud, Ahmad Shah (1953–2001). Prominent Afghan commander who was highly regarded for his role in driving the Soviets out of Afghanistan, earning him the name "The Lion of Panjshir." He was of Tajik descent, and he was a Kabul University engineering student who became a prominent Afghan military leader. He became the leader of the United Islamic Front for the Salvation of Afghanistan and was assassinated by al-Qaeda agents on September 9, 2001, and was later declared a national hero for his efforts in Afghanistan.

Rabbani, Burhanuddin (1940–). Former president of Afghanistan from 1992 to 1996 until he was ousted by the Taliban invasion in Kabul. He is the leader of Jamiat-e Islami Afghanistan, also known as the Islamic Society of Afghanistan. Rabbani also served as the leader of the United Islamic Front for the Salvation of Afghanistan, which allied with various political groups against the Taliban regime.

Samar, Sima (1957–). The first deputy chair and minister of women's affairs in Afghanistan, she is currently the chairperson of the Afghanistan Independent Human Rights Commission. She is a pioneer for women's rights in Afghanistan, refusing to accept that women must be kept secluded from the public, and speaks out against wearing the burqa garment. Under the Taliban regime, women were required to wear the burqa and be covered from head to toe, and many women in Afghanistan today suffer from osteomalacia, a softening of the bones due to an insufficient diet and a lack of sunlight.

Seleucus Nicator I (358 B.C.E.–281 B.C.E.). A Macedonian general under Alexander the Great, he participated in the revolt and assassination of Perdiccas that resulted in the division of Alexander's empire into four large territories. Seleucus gained control Alexander's lands in the east, and thus began the Seleucid Empire in Afghanistan. After signing a treaty with the Mauryan dynasty, Seleucus ceded all lands south of the Hindu Kush Mountains.

Shah, Mohammad Nadir (1880–1933). King of Afghanistan from 1929 to 1933. He reversed all of King Amunella's reforms and reinstated traditional values. During his reign, thousands were killed, imprisoned, or forced to flee to the Soviet Union.

Shah, Timur (1748–1793). The second son of Ahmad Shah Durrani, he assumed the throne on his father's death in 1772. Previously overthrown after his father left him in control of India in 1757, under his rule as king, the Durrani Empire began to crumble. In 1776, Timur Shah Durrani was forced to move the capital from Kandahar and established Kabul as the capital of Afghanistan.

Shah, Zahir (1914–). Zahir Shah has the distinct honor of being the youngest, longest-serving, and last king of Afghanistan. He ruled from 1933 to 1973 until he was ousted in a bloodless coup by former Prime Minister Daoud and forced into exile in Italy. Most notably during his reign, he ratified the 1964 Constitution and implemented multiple political and economic reforms for the country.

Taraki, Nur Mohammad (1913–1979). Afghan political figure and founder of the People's Democratic Party of Afghanistan. Taraki was also a leader in the political coup in April 1978 that ousted President Daoud, after which Taraki assumed power as the president of Afghanistan from 1978 to 1979. He implemented radical Marxist policies and challenged traditional Afghan values under the Khalq regime until he was overthrown in 1979.

Tarzi, Soraya (1899–1968). As the wife of King Amanullah Khan, Queen Soraya Tarzi was the political face of championing women's independence in Afghanistan, and she was also the daughter of Mahmud Tarzi. She was a pioneer in the women's rights movement in Afghanistan, and she was a devout supporter of the enlightenment period for women. Her efforts have often given her the distinction of being the first and one of the most powerful Afghani female activists. Her feminine advancement efforts included education for females and the inclusion of women in political activities. She is the only female ruler of Afghanistan, as the king credited her as the minister of education in Afghanistan. She was the first female ruler to appear in public without her veiled facial covering, and many of her actions and efforts were deemed too progressive for antiquated Afghanistan.

Zoroaster. Iranian prophet and founder of the Middle East religion called Zoroastrianism. His date of birth is highly debated, with estimates ranging from 1200 B.C.E. to 600 B.C.E. His religious beliefs were influential in Afghanistan after the conversion of King Vishtaspa, believed to have occurred in the fifth century B.C.E.

Glossary of Frequently Used Terms

Afridi: A powerful and dominant Pashtun tribe located in eastern Afghanistan in the region of the Khyber Pass. The Afridi are divided into eight clans and are well known for their part in the 1895 Khyber Rifles.

Aimaq (Aimak): A seminomadic ethnic group living in the northwestern highlands of Afghanistan, located immediately north of Herat.

Allah: The word for God in Arabic and the term for the only deity in Islam.

Amir (emir): Term used as a high title of nobility or office, such as commander or ruler.

azaan: The Islamic call for the five daily prayers.

badal: The Pashtun law of revenge.

bad-dadan: The custom by which a woman was given away in marriage to compensate for a crime.

baksheesh: A Middle Eastern term of several meanings that can describe a charitable contribution to beggars, a tip as a sign of gratitude or respect, or a bribe paid to corrupt government officials.

Barakzai: A major sect of the Pashtun clan, notably a subtribe of the Durrani Pashtuns, descendants of which have ruled as kings since 1835.

buzkashi: A traditional Afghan game played on horseback in which the headless carcass of a calf or goat is the object sought after by the opposing teams.

chadar (chadari): The traditional veiled clothing for women to wear in public worn by Pashtun women in Afghanistan. The chadari has a mesh opening for the eyes and is worn over regular clothing. This is different than the Afghan burqa, which covers a woman's facial features so that she is completely covered from head to toe.

Dari: A dialect of the Persian language spoken mainly in Afghanistan and known locally as Farsi.

Dupatta: A long shawl or scarf worn by women around the head or neck and worn when dressed in shalwar kameez.

Durrani: The Durrani line has been the source of Afghanistan's kings since Ahmad Shah Durrani in 1747; the descendants have come from either the Saddozi line or the Barakzai line.

e'dam: Afghan term for capital punishment.

emam: Term used to describe a religious leader.

fakir: A holy man, one who is a Sufi, and especially one who performs unbelievable or magical acts, often used to refer to a spiritual recluse or a beggar.

Farsi: Local name for one of the two main languages spoken in Afghanistan and of Persian dialect.

Farsiwan: An ethnic group in western Afghanistan, they are a subgroup to the Tajiks and are distinguished generally by their following of Shi'a Islam.

feringhee: Term used to describe a foreigner.

Gandamak, Treaty of: Treaty signed on May 26, 1879, by the Afghans and the British to officially end the Second Anglo-Afghan War. The treaty gave the British control of Afghan territory and would prevent further invasion in the country, but many Afghan people saw it as a humiliation.

ghaza: A type of holy war and used as a term for battle.

Ghilzai: One of the two largest groups of the Pashtun tribe of eastern and northern Afghanistan and the most populous Pashtun tribe in Afghanistan.

Hajj: The pilgrimage to Mecca, one of five Muslim religious duties and a rite of passage in Islam.

Hanafi: The oldest of the four major schools of Islamic law within Sunni Islam. It is dominant among more than 80 percent of the Sunni population in Afghanistan.

Hazara: An ethnic group residing in the mountains of central Afghanistan, mostly of Mongolian origin.

hejab: The Taliban enforcement of the seclusion of women from society.

hoquq-i-zanan: Term that refers to women's rights.

hudud: Term to describe the Islamic law rules of social behavior and the penalties for crimes, including severe punishment for acts such as theft, including amputations.

jaza: Term for punishment.

jihad: Religious holy war and struggle in defense of Islam against attackers or infidels.

jirga: An assembly of tribal elders or leaders.

Kalashnikovization: Term used to describe the lawlessness during the 1980s and 1990s due to the use and availability of the AK-47 assault rifle.

khan: A title used to mean lord of chief and is considered an elite title of respect.

Khyber Pass: An important and historic pass connecting Pakistan to the Afghan border. Historically, it has been a vital trade route and strategic military location.

Khyber Rifles: A paramilitary corps during the British rule comprised of members of the Afridi tribe and the Pakistani army that protected the Khyber Pass.

loya jirga: A tradition that is at least 1,000 years old, the term describes a grand assembly or great council as a large meeting. Participants include great political, military, and religious leaders. There are no time limits, and the meeting is held until a consensus is reached.

madrassa: The Arabic word for school, usually in reference to an Islamic schoolhouse or college.

mahr: A tradition in Islamic marriage, it is a marriage offering from the groom to the bride and is a gift only for her, not for her father.

masjid: A mosque or a place of worship in the Islamic faith.

Meli Shura: The highest legislative body in Afghanistan.

mujahideen (mujahedin): Arabic term for holy warriors of Islam in the Middle East. In Afghanistan, the mujahideen refers to the Afghan opposition groups that fought against the Soviet invasion from 1979 to 1989.

mullah: A religious priest or teacher on Islamic rules and traditions known as Islamic clergy.

naan: A popular bread item for food, it is a round flatbread similar to pita and is a staple item to hot meals in Afghanistan.

Namaaz (salat): Refers to ritual prayers said five times daily by Islamic followers.

namus: An ethical term for men and households in Afghanistan, it describes the defense of the honor of women in the household.

Pashtun (Pushtun): A major ethnic tribe living in eastern and southern Afghanistan characterized by their Pashto language and their following of Pashtunwali.

Pashtunwali: A pre-Islamic religious code of honor.

Powindah: Term to describe an Afghan nomad.

Pushto: One of the two main languages spoken in Afghanistan, mainly by the people in southeastern Afghanistan.

qarez: An underground aqueduct system unique to Afghanistan and Iran.

Qur'an (Koran): The sacred book of Islam.

rajm: An Arabic term that means "to stone" as a punishment for adultery.

Ramadan (Ramazan): The Fourth Pillar of Islam, it is a monthlong period of religious fasting from sunrise to sunset where purity of action and thought are observed throughout the day.

Rawalpindi, Treaty of: A peace treaty signed by the United Kingdom and Afghanistan on August 8, 1919, at the end of the Third Anglo-Afghan War. The terms of the treaty gave Afghanistan independence, established that the British Empire would not extend beyond the Khyber Pass, and ceased British subsidies into Afghanistan.

sabnamah: Term refers to "night letters" that were distributed at night and tucked under the door of people's houses, containing antigovernment or anti-Taliban statements.

Salat: The Second Pillar of Islam that calls for ritual prayers or worship.

sarkar (sirkar): Term used to describe the government or a historical administrative unit.

satrap: In ancient history, a term originated by Cyrus the Great, this is the given name of the governors of the empire's provinces. Alexander the Great revised the satrap system when his Macedonian army conquered the Persians and reduced the satrap powers of such authority as commanding the troops and issuing coinage. In modern times, the term is also used to describe world leaders who are influenced by larger world superpowers.

Sawm: The Third Pillar of Islam, it is the act of fasting during the month of Ramadan.

sayyid: Honorific title given to Afghanistan's holy men and traditional healers.

Shahadat: The First Pillar of Islam, it is the belief that Allah is the only God and that his messenger is the Prophet Muhammad.

Sharia: The body of Islamic law.

Simla Manifesto: Declaration of war in 1838 that marked the start of the First Anglo-Afghan War, sent by Lord Auckland to Afghanistan.

Sunni: A major Islamic sect that represents more than 80 percent of Afghanistan's population.

Tajik: A major ethnic group in northeastern Afghanistan and in the cities of Kabul, Mazari Sharif, and Herat.

talib (taleb): The Arabic word for a student of a madrassa school.

Taliban (Taleban): An extreme Islamic fundamentalist group that effectively overthrew Afghanistan in 1996 and remained in control until 2001. The term is a plural form of the word *talib* and represents students of religious madrassas in Pakistan and Afghanistan.

Uzbek: One of the major ethnic groups in Afghanistan located in the plains. They are primarily farmers and herders.

velayat: An administrative division or province.

wazir (vizier): Literally meaning "burden bearer" in Persian, this refers to a high-ranking political or religious adviser to a Muslim monarch.

Wolasi Jirgah: The House of Representatives in Afghanistan.

Zakat: The Fourth Pillar of Islam, it refers to the paying of alms or giving to the poor.

Works Referenced and Suggested Further Readings

The author has included books that have been referenced or cited while writing *The History of Afghanistan*. Included are those books that are readily available in most libraries or on the Internet. These texts may also be helpful for those interested in exploring more details on the topics presented in this book.

Aizenman, N. C. "Afghan Jew Becomes Country's One and Only." *Washington Post*, January 27, 2005, A10.

Armstrong, Sally. *Veiled Threat: The Hidden Power of the Women of Afghanistan.* New York: Four Walls Eight Windows Publishing, 2002.

Bernard, Cheryl. *Veiled Courage: Inside the Afghan Women's Resistance.* New York: Broadway Books, 2002.

Bowen, Donna Lee, and Evelyn A. Early. *Everyday Life in the Muslim Middle East.* 2nd ed. Bloomington: Indiana University Press, 2002.

Briant, Pierre. *Alexander the Great: Man of Action, Man of Spirit.* New York: Harry N. Abrams, 1996.

Cantor, Norman F., with Dee Ranieri. *Alexander the Great: Journey to the End of the Earth.* New York: HarperCollins, 2005.

Constable, Pamela. "A Poor Yield for Afghans' War on Drugs." *Washington Post Foreign Service*, September 19, 2006, A14.

Cool, Steve. *Ghost Wars: The Secret History of the CIA, Afghanistan, and bin Laden, from the Soviet Invasion to September 10, 2001*. New York: Penguin, 2004.

Cooley, John K. *Unholy Wars: Afghanistan, America, and International Terrorism.* 2nd ed. Sterling, Va.: Pluto Press, 2000.

Dixon, Norm. "How the CIA Created Osama bin Laden." *Green Left Weekly,* September 19, 2001, issue no. 465.

Dupree, Louis. *Shamshir Ghar: Historic Cave Site in Kandahar Province, Afghanistan.* Anthropological Papers of the American Museum of Natural History 46, no. 2. New York: American Museum of Natural History, 1958.

———, et al. "Prehistoric Research in Afghanistan (1959–1966)." *Transactions of the American Philosophical Society,* n.s., 62, no. 4 (1972):1–84.

Dupree, Nancy. "An Historical Guide to Afghanistan." Afghan Tourist Organization. 1970. http://www.zharov.com/dupree/chapter23.html

Emadi, Hafizullah. *Culture and Customs of Afghanistan.* Westport, Conn.: Greenwood Press, 2005.

Ewans, Martin. *Afghanistan: A Short History of Its People and Politics.* New York: HarperCollins, 2002.

Farahi, Abdul G. *Afghanistan during Democracy and Republic: 1963–1978.* Translated by Juma Khan Sufi. Kabul: UNO Education Press, 2004.

Gall, Carlotta. "Record Opium Crop Possible in Afghanistan, U.N. Study Predicts." *New York Times,* March 6, 2007, A12.

Gohari, M. J. *The Taliban: Ascent to Power.* Oxford: Oxford University Press, 2001.

Goldschmidt, Arthur, Jr. *A Concise History of the Middle East.* 7th ed. Cambridge: Westview Press, 2002.

Goodson, Larry P. *Afghanistan's Endless War: State Failure, Regional Politics, and the Rise of the Taliban.* Seattle: University of Washington Press, 2001.

Griffin, Michael. *Reaping the Whirlwind: Afghanistan, Al-Qa'ida and the Holy War.* Sterling, Va.: Pluto Press, 2003.

Hildinger, Erik. *Warriors of the Steppe: A Military History of Central Asia, 500 B.C. to 1700 A.D.* New York: Sarpedon, 1997.

Hopkirk, Peter. *The Great Game: The Struggle for Empire in Central Asia.* Reprint, New York: Kodansha America, Inc., 1994. (First published in Great Britain in 1990 as *The Great Game: On Secret Service in High Asia* by John Murray Publishers, Ltd.)

Jones, Ann. *Kabul in Winter: Life without Peace in Afghanistan.* New York: Metropolitan Books, 2006.

Kaplan, Robert D. "Afghanistan Postmortem." *Atlantic Monthly* 263, no. 4 (April 1989): 26–29.

———. "The Coming Anarchy." *Atlantic Monthly* 273, no. 2 (February 1994): 44–76.

——. "The Lawless Frontier." *Atlantic Monthly* 286, no. 3 (September 2000): 66–80.

——. *Soldiers of God: With Islamic Warriors in Afghanistan and Pakistan.* New York: Vintage Departures Edition, 2001.

Keegan, John. "The Ordeal of Afghanistan." *Atlantic Monthly* 256, no. 5 (November 1985): 94–105.

Lewis, Bernard. *The Middle East: A Brief History of the Last 2,000 Years.* New York: Scribner, 1995.

Maley, William, ed. *Fundamentalism Reborn? Afghanistan and the Taliban.* New York: New York University Press, 2001.

Maloney, Sean M. *Enduring the Freedom: A Rogue Historian in Afghanistan.* Washington, D.C.: Potomac Books, 2005.

Man, John. *Genghis Khan: Life, Death, and Resurrection.* New York: Thomas Dunne Books of St. Martin's Press, 2004.

Mansfield, Peter. *A History of the Middle East.* New York: Viking, 1991.

Margolis, Eric S. *War at the Top of the World: The Struggle for Afghanistan, Kashmir, and Tibet.* New York: Routledge, 2000.

Marozzi, Justin. *Tamerlane: Sword of Islam, Conqueror of the World.* Cambridge: De Capo Press, 2004.

Marsden, Peter. *The Taliban: War, Religion and the New Order in Afghanistan.* New York: St. Martin's Press, 1998.

Mason, Colin. *A Short History of Asia: Stone Age to 2000 A.D.* New York: St. Martin's Press, 2000.

Meyer, Karl. *The Dust of Empire: The Race for Mastery in the Asian Heartland.* New York: The Century Foundation, 2003.

Moore, Robin. *The Hunt for Bin Laden: Task Force Dagger.* New York: Random House, 2003.

Morgan, David. *The Mongols.* Cambridge: Blackwell Publishers, 1986.

Myrdal, Jan, and Gun Kessle. *Gates to Asia: A Diary from a Long Journey.* New York: Pantheon Books, 1971.

Nawid, Senzil K. *Religious Response to Social Change in Afghanistan 1919–29.* Costa Mesa, Calif.: Mazda Publishers, 1999.

Nojumi, Neamatollah. *The Rise of the Taliban in Afghanistan: Mass Mobilization, Civil War, and the Future of the Region.* New York: Palgrave, 2002.

Randal, Jonathan. *Osama: The Making of a Terrorist.* New York: Knopf, 2004.

Rashid, Ahmed. *Taliban: Militant Islam, Oil, and Fundamentalism in Central Asia.* New Haven, Conn.: Yale University Press, 2000.

Roy, Oliver. *Islam and Resistance in Afghanistan.* 2nd ed. Cambridge: Cambridge University Press, 1990.

Rubin, Barnett R. *The Fragmentation of Afghanistan: State Formation and Collapse in the International System.* 2nd ed. New Haven, Conn.: Yale University Press, 2002.

Russel, Malcolm B., and Ray Cleveland. *The Middle East and South Asia: Afghanistan.* 39th ed. Harpers Ferry, W.Va.: Stryker-Post Publications, 2005.

Sarin, Oleg, and Lev Dvoretsky. *The Afghan Syndrome: The Soviet Union's Vietnam.* Novato, Calif.: Presidio Press, 1993.

Smucker, Philip. "Taliban Talks Open Rift in Kabul Leadership." *Washington Times,* April 9, 2007, A10.

Stewart, Jules. *The Khyber Rifles: From the British Raj to Al Qaeda.* Stroud: Sutton Publishing, 2005.

Stossel, Sage. "Understanding Afghanistan." *Atlantic Monthly* 288, no. 3 (October 2001): 87–90.

Stroup, Herbert. *Founders of Living Religions.* Philadelphia: Westminster Press, 1974.

Tang, Alisa. "1,423 Secured Afghan Artifacts Are Returned to Kabul Museum." *San Diego Union Tribune,* March 18, 2007. http://www.signon sandiego.com/uniontrib/20070318/news_1n18afghan.html.

Tanner, Stephen. *Afghanistan: A Military History from Alexander the Great to the Fall of the Taliban.* New York: Da Capo Press, 2002.

Thapar, Romila. *Asoka and the Decline of the Mauryas.* New York: Oxford University Press, 1960.

Weatherford, Jack McIver. *Ghengis Khan and the Making of the Modern World.* New York: Crown Publishers, 2004.

Weaver, Mary Anne. *Pakistan: In the Shadow of Jihad and Afghanistan.* New York: Farrar, Straus & Giroux, 2002.

Wimmel, Kenneth. *The Alluring Target: In Search of the Secrets of Central Asia.* Fairfax, Va.: Trackless Sands Press, 1996.

Woodward, John, ed. *Afghanistan: Opposing Viewpoints.* Detroit: Greenhaven Press, 2006.

Yousaf, Mohammad, and Mark Adkin. *Afghanistan—The Bear Trap: The Defeat of a Superpower.* Havertown, Penn.: Casemate, 2001.

Index

About the Author

MEREDITH L. RUNION is a Program Manager for the Federal Government.

Other Titles in the Greenwood Histories of the Modern Nations
Frank W. Thackeray and John E. Findling, Series Editors

The History of Argentina
Daniel K. Lewis

The History of Australia
Frank G. Clarke

The History of the Baltic States
Kevin O'Connor

The History of Brazil
Robert M. Levine

The History of Canada
Scott W. See

The History of Central America
Thomas Pearcy

The History of Chile
John L. Rector

The History of China
David C. Wright

The History of Congo
Didier Gondola

The History of Cuba
Clifford L. Staten

The History of Egypt
Glenn E. Perry

The History of Ethiopia
Saheed Adejumobi

The History of Finland
Jason Lavery

The History of France
W. Scott Haine

The History of Germany
Eleanor L. Turk

The History of Ghana
Roger S. Gocking

The History of Great Britain
Anne Baltz Rodrick

The History of Holland
Mark T. Hooker

The History of India
John McLeod

The History of Indonesia
Steven Drakeley

The History of Iran
Elton L. Daniel

The History of Iraq
Courtney Hunt

The History of Ireland
Daniel Webster Hollis III

The History of Israel
Arnold Blumberg

The History of Italy
Charles L. Killinger

The History of Japan
Louis G. Perez

The History of Korea
Djun Kil Kim

The History of Kuwait
Michael S. Casey

The History of Mexico
Burton Kirkwood

The History of New Zealand
Tom Brooking